AF323208

SOUNDS – MEANING – COMMUNICATION

LANDMARKS IN PHONETICS, PHONOLOGY AND COGNITIVE LINGUISTICS

Edited by Jolanta Szpyra-Kozłowska

VOLUME 3

Notes on the quality assurance and peer review of this publication

Prior to publication, the quality of the work published in this series is reviewed by an external referee appointed by the editorship.

Angelina Żyśko

English
'Joyful' Vocabulary –
Semantic Developments

Bibliographic Information published by the Deutsche Nationalbibliothek
The Deutsche Nationalbibliothek lists this publication in the Deutsche
Nationalbibliografie; detailed bibliographic data is available in the internet
at http://dnb.d-nb.de.

This publication was financially supported by
Maria Curie-Skłodowska University, Lublin, Poland.

Cover illustration printed with kind permission of Jerzy Durczak.

Reviewed by Adam Głaz.

ISSN 2365-8150
ISBN 978-3-631-66919-8 (Print)
E-ISBN 978-3-653-06447-6 (E-PDF)
E-ISBN 978-3-631-70149-2 (EPUB)
E-ISBN 978-3-631-70150-8 (MOBI)
DOI 10.3726/978-3-653-06447-6

© Peter Lang GmbH
Internationaler Verlag der Wissenschaften
Frankfurt am Main 2016
All rights reserved.
Peter Lang Edition is an Imprint of Peter Lang GmbH.

Peter Lang – Frankfurt am Main · Bern · Bruxelles · New York ·
Oxford · Warszawa · Wien

This publication has been peer reviewed.

www.peterlang.com

Contents

List of Abbreviations

a	(in dates) ante
btasd	Bosworth-Toller Anglo-Saxon Dictionary (http://bosworth.ff.cuni.cz/)
c.	(in dates) circa
cyberhymnal	hymntime (http://www.cyberhymnal.org/htm/j/t/jthoujoy.htm)
dictionary	online English dictionary (http://dictionary.reference.com)
Du.	Dutch
Eng.	English
E.OE	Early Old English
Fr.	French
Fris.	Frisian
Ger.	German
GDSQ	Gaither's Dictionary of Scientific Quotations
glp	German Lexicon Project (http://www.ling.upenn.edu/~kurisuto/germanic/language_resources.html)
Lat.	Latin
LDCE	Longman Dictionary of Contemporary English
LDOCE 5	Longman Dictionary of Contemporary English, 5th edition
med	Middle English Dictionary (http://quod.lib.umich.edu/m/med/)
MidDu	Middle Dutch
MidE	Middle English (1066–1450/1500)
ModE	Modern English (1450/1500>)
m-w	Merriam-Webster Dictionary http://www.merriam-webster.com/dictionary
NT	Nowy Testament. New Testament
odo	Oxford Dictionaries (http://oxforddictionaries.com/)
OE	Old English (449–1066)
OED	Oxford English Dictionary
oed	Oxford English Dictionary (http://www.oed.com/)
OFr	Old French
OFris	Old Frisian
OHG	Old High German
ON	Old Norse

online ed	Online Etymology Dictionary (http://www.etymonline.com/)
OS	Old Saxon
OSl.	Old Church Slavonic
spurgeongems	Charles Spurgeon (www.spurgeongems.org)
tfd	the Free Dictionary (http://www.thefreedictionary.com/)

List of Figures

List of Tables

Introduction

In this book, an attempt is made to explain how and why word senses are brought together within the bounds of single words. The present project, then, is meant to be a contribution to the problem of what it actually is that serves as an organiser of the lexicon. There seem to be good reasons to assume that there must be some explanation for the fact that (i) words expand by developing newer and newer senses, and that (ii) words can be brought together into semantic sets. On a more general level, as John Chrysostom states, "(…) there is nothing that has been created without some reason, even if human nature is incapable of knowing precisely the reason for them all" (in: *GDSQ* 2008). A contemporary expression of this position can be found in Langacker (2008: 10): "cognitive and functional linguists find that virtually everything in language is motivated (…) (even if very little is strictly predictable)". More specifically, the book is written within the spirit of ideology of two linguists: Langacker's philosophy of language, cognition and domains (1987, 1988, 1990, 1991, 1994, 1998, 1999, 2002, 2008, 2009, 2011a, 2011b, 2015), and Łozowski's understanding of panchrony (1993, 1999, 2000, 2005, 2008, 2010, 2011, 2012a, 2012b, 2012c, 2014).

First and foremost, it is Langacker's (ibid.) vision of language and cognition, and more importantly, the understanding of cognitive/conceptual domains that is the key issue in this book. Dealing with words, one needs to be aware that linguistic meaning comprises of conceptual content and the construal imposed on the content, where the construal is understood as the ability to conceive and portray the same situation in alternative ways (Langacker 2008: 43–44). According to Langacker (2008: 44), an expression or a word invokes a set of cognitive domains as "(…) the basis for its meaning (i.e. as the content to be construed)". In other words, a domain may be understood as any kind of conception or realm of experience. Of course, if a word or an expression invokes more that one domain, i.e. a set of domains, it is said to invoke a matrix of domains. If this is so, then our understanding of the world has much to do with cognitive/conceptual domains, as we as people tend to experience the world every day, and having done so, we tend to give our experiences a particular name, i.e. we want to find an appropriate word with an appropriate meaning thanks to which we can talk/think about what we experience in our lives. Consequently, if we cannot find such words, our human nature tells us to use an already existing word with a slightly different shade of meaning. After all, people's associations are various and individualised, e.g. when thinking about/ contemplating/reading about/etc. the moon one person can associate it with the celestial body, while another person may think of love/romantic relationships/etc. Those associations of ours depend on our experience. Hence, it is our experience that influences cognition and, as a result, all the other processes that result from cognition, language change being one of them.

The other linguist whose philosophy is of utmost importance in the present book is Łozowski (ibid.), whose vision of panchrony stands for the key philosophy of meaning change in this book. According to Łozowski (ibid.), words change their meanings for certain (linguistic or extra-linguistic) reasons. In other words, the process of language change and, at the same time, meaning change, is motivated by cognitive processes in the human mind. Łozowski (2008: 79) claims that, although it is cognitive factors that are language variables, language still exists in relation to space-time reality: a) owing to its semantic character, language mirrors spatio-temporal realia, b) owing to its symbolic nature, language can transform time and space, the process resulting in a linguistic picture of the world (or world-view), and c) due to its anthropological character, language is a function of cognition. Hence, in the words of Łozowski (ibid.), panchrony, understood as language change plus cognition, is "a way of thinking of language in terms of experiential, relative, and subjective projections" (Łozowski 2008: 79). Panchrony, unlike diachrony, as viewed by the linguist, is not only about functioning in space and time, but, most importantly, about operating in human understanding. Thus, what makes panchrony different from diachrony is the motivating factors that stand behind language semantic change: "language change is motivated historically in diachrony and cognitively in panchrony, and (…) the space-time continuum plays the role of a language variable in diachrony and of a derivative of cognition in panchrony" (Łozowski 2008:79).

Therefore, by joining Langacker's philosophy of language, cognition and, most importantly, of cognitive/conceptual domains with Łozowski's idea of panchrony, I want to obtain a cognitive picture of language, and especially of meaning change. It is not words that change their meanings because of historical/linguistic/cultural/etc. reasons, but it is we, as human beings, that change the meanings of words due to our cognition.

The aim of the present book is to identify and explore the parameters that seem to be responsible for grouping words and bringing their meanings together, which amounts to a search for the motivating forces, processes, mechanisms, tools, and measures behind historical semantic changes in selected English vocabulary. As these parameters can be either of intra-linguistic or extra-linguistic nature, we need to include both structural and functional perspectives in our search.

According to the adherents of the structural approach towards language, words are brought together into semantic fields. According to Trier (1931), a semantic field is a structured set of interdependent words. Because there are many lexical items in a semantic field, they enter into all kinds of relations with one another, one word being linked with more than one of its neighbours or with words from other semantic fields. The relations, paradigmatic and syntagmatic in character, determine the word's position within a semantic field and, consequently, its meaning. Hence, a change of one element in a semantic field causes a change in the neighbouring ones.

However, one question that arises is whether relations between lexical items can be treated as the only parameters that shape word meaning. In contrast to this view, the present work is based on the assumption that language is not autonomous, but rather integrated with a variety of extra-linguistic factors. This brings us to the functionally-oriented cognitive approach to language. In the words of John Taylor,

> [r]ather than regard language as an autonomous component of the mind (…) language study is shaped from the outset by what is believed to be cognitively plausible. The best assumption, therefore, is that language is best regarded as an integral part of cognition, and that it will be insightful to study language in light of what is known about the mind, whether this be from experimentation, introspection, or even common-sense observation. (Taylor 2002: 8)

Putting it differently, language resides in thought. Thought, in turn, depends on an individual's experience, culture, tradition, mental associations, impressions, etc. To be more precise, meaning resides in conceptualisation, which is rooted in physical reality and social interaction. Since meaning is based on the interlocutors' thoughts, intentions and knowledge, it is negotiated during human interaction. Therefore, I postulate that the search for the motivating principles of word sets be carried out within the framework of cognitive, rather than structural, linguistics. For this reason, I consider cognitive domains, not semantic fields, to be the environment that organises vocabulary, a cognitive domain being understood as "a more generalised 'background' knowledge configuration against which conceptualisation is achieved" (Taylor 2002: 195).

One logical implication of this approach is that

> (…) words must be taken as symbols of human experience of the world: quite like national emblems (the Polish white-tailed eagle, the British lion, the Swedish three crowns, the Australian golden wattle), social and religious tokens and conventions (the wedding ring, the Christian cross, the Islamic crescent and star), or even omens (the black cat, the raven, the lightning), words are forms that have been given their meaning

> proportionately to the experience of those who find the given form-meaning correlation
> absolutely justified and necessary. (Łozowski 2012a: 1–2)

Words and their meanings are not lexical relations generated arbitrarily by a self-regulating linguistic system, but, as Łozowski continues, "every single word is an accumulative record of the subsequent layers of the self-awareness that the past and present generations of speakers did and do find relevant enough to self-express" (ibid., p. 2). For this reason, word meanings cannot be said to be purely synchronic or diachronic, but they must be *panchronic,* i.e. cross-generational (cf. Łozowski 1999, 2008, 2011). In practice, our cultural experience of the world we live in results in mental projections we make of the world. Some of these projections, or conceptualisations, wholly or partly, happen to be reflected in language. If this is the case, each of the resulting linguistic expressions stands for some aspect of the experience that triggered the whole process of conceptualising the world.

This book is an invitation to discover the relevant aspects of human experience that, over the centuries, have motivated semantic developments in selected English vocabulary. I hope, then, to be able to provide a cognitive linguistic contribution to the program that Geeraerts (2010: 14) ascribes to the 19[th]century historical-philological school of linguistics: "[to] try to understand (…) the cultural forms of expression in which men [i.e. people] have, throughout history, laid down their experience of the world".

Acknowledgements

Several people have earned my deepest gratitude for the help, encouragement and professional assistance they offered while I was writing this book. My sincere thanks therefore go, firstly, to Professor Przemysław Łozowski (UMCS Lublin). I am deeply grateful for all his comments, discussions and suggestions without which the present study would not have been completed. I also wish to thank Professor Henryk Kardela (UMCS Lublin), Professor Jolanta Szpyra-Kozłowska (UMCS Lublin), Professor Adam Głaz (UMCS Lublin), and Professor Małgorzata Fabiszak (UAM Poznań) for their valuable comments and ideas which enriched the book. On a more personal note, I owe a special debt of gratitude to those who are dear to me. I wish to thank my husband Konrad, whose motivation, help and belief in me were invaluable. I also cannot miss the opportunity to express my gratitude to my parents and sister, who have always supported and believed in me. All shortcomings are, of course, my own responsibility.

Chapter 1: Semantic Fields and Diachrony

1.1 Introduction

Words do not function in isolation, but are grouped in various ways in the mental lexicon. According to Keyser (1927: 94), "[t]o be is to be related". Therefore, in order to exist, a word needs to enter into a variety of relations with other words. The advocates of the structural approach to language maintain that the notion of semantic fields serves as a linguistic parameter for bringing vocabulary together. Because semantic fields can be studied from the diachronic perspective, they can apparently offer a complete linguistic picture of lexical groups, revealing information about the roots of lexical items and their relations with other words. The present chapter mainly examines the ways of grouping vocabulary, outlines the development of the field theory, as well as considers its issues from the perspective of the latest postulates in contemporary semantics. Furthermore, not only does this chapter deal with different controversial aspects associated with the notion of semantic fields, focusing on the issue of field boundaries and membership, but it also aims to systematise field terminology. This is necessary because a variety of terms have been applied to refer to the same concept by different authors.

Language changes both in space and time: it is in constant flux. Meanings of words change when people start using them with reference to new denotata; they narrow or broaden their range of application, they undergo amelioration or pejoration etc. Lexemes disappear and new ones enter the lexicon, but the relationship between them also constantly changes. We look below at semantic alterations as they are studied within the framework of structurally oriented diachronic semantics, an approach that focuses on language change over time. All in all, the major objective of this chapter is to show how the theory of semantic fields is related to the concept of diachronic semantics, i.e to the theory of description, not explanation, of language change over time.

1.2 Jost Trier: the cradle of field theory

The diachronic study of meaning, drawing from structuralism, presupposes that words are grouped into semantic or lexical fields. Traditionally, Jost Trier's (1931) name is commonly associated with the beginnings of semantic field theory. Although Kleparski and Rusinek (2007a: 76, 2007b: 189) trace its roots back to the aforementioned linguist, the ideas of the German scholar did have their predecessors, whose contributions to the study of semantic field were so immense as to influence even contemporary approaches. For example, Vassilyev (1974: 79) finds the stimulus to the semantic field approach in Meyer's (1910: 352–368) proposals, while Öhman (1951: 73) discovers that this issue was also dealt by Tegnér (1874). Allan (2001: 258) and Murphy (2003: 67), on the other hand, trace the notion of semantic fields back to Humboldt (1836). However, what seems to be most surprising is the fact that the cradle of the idea may be found in Antiquity, for ancient philosophers had already noticed that nature is organised into what can be called fields (for instance, Plato referred to the principle of organic unity; cf. Rousseau 1972: 20).

There is evidence that the father of the very first, and apparently not very sophisticated semantic field system, was the Catalonian medieval poet and philosopher Raymondus Lullus (born around 1235; cf. Llull 1645/1970). He is also known as Ramón Llull, and he attempted to create a logical system encompassing all fields of knowledge (cf. Wildgen 2000: 204–211). He joined a few conceptual systems, arranged in a linear order, with nine segments, into a circular field so that every concept had two neighbours. He then decided to add particular figures inside, with the aim of creating a sub-network of concepts. In addition, more specific fields were incorporated into the universal field, including the most elementary life qualities, which resembles the contemporary cognitive attitude towards field theory.

Fig. 1. Llull's semantic field (1645/1970).

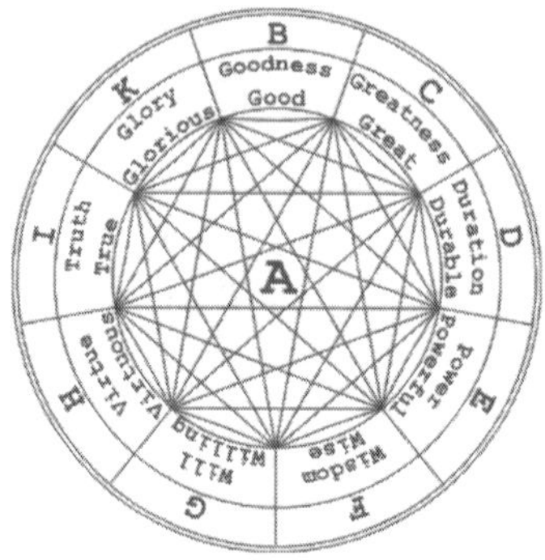

It is interesting to note that Llull did not stop at the idea of a static conceptual field. He went further in his analysis, explaining the possible causes of language change. Thus, via the rotation of the circles and the consequent change of neighbouring elements, what he proposed could be referred to as the dynamic character of a semantic field. As a result, a combination of simple morphemes could generate complex morphemes on a morphological level, and combinations of words could bring about phrases and sentences according to their syntactic interpretation. This is especially relevant for our purposes – these processes could result in language changes.

Llull's impact on the study of language, although somewhat forgotten, was a momentous event. Hence, we are justified in supporting Wildgen (2000: 207, 206), who, although criticising Llull's system of semantic fields as

> at first sight very primitive, and its dynamics are extremely crude, for they lack the necessary restriction of a free algebra, which is characteristic of generative systems in Chomsky's sense

is aware that

> the ideas/concepts/words from linear arrays, that the extremes may be glued together, and that a hierarchy of such arrays exists, is a first realization of 'field-semantics'.

With similar general considerations in mind, I find it surprising that almost all publications on field theory do not refer to the work of Lull or Giordano Bruno (see below). Hence, there are grounds to state that Wildgen (2000: 203–226) is an eye-opener when it comes to the real beginnings of what is now known as semantic field theory.

The second half of the 16th century witnessed an elaboration of Lullian circular fields. This was due to the fact that Giordano Bruno (1591/1991), an Italian Renaissance philosopher, having based his approach on the analogy between the macrocosm (the universe) and the microcosm (the human being), replaced Llull's closed linear field with a regular, bi-dimensional pattern extending to infinity.[1]

According to Bruno, a field should have a regular surface filled with other regular or circular surfaces. Bruno's proposal resembles an atrium-like house that stands for an early version of a semantic field. The scholar assumed that the filling of a surface with squares tends to be the most appropriate in terms of the organisation of a conceptual system, the central room of the house staying open and the remaining eight rooms being in its periphery. Thus, presupposing the homogenous character of all the eight fields mentioned above, it should come as no surprise that such a system tends to have both static and dynamic aspects. While the static character focuses only on the types of semantic relations between the sub-fields, the most prominent relations being spatial, part-whole or focus-periphery,[2] the issue

---

1 The issue of infinity plays a huge role in Giordano Bruno's philosophy. This is confirmed by Łąkowski (1983: 373), who portrays Bruno as a person who "perceived nature as an infinite, dynamic entity and proposed a dialectic outline of its evolution".

2 It should be mentioned in connection with this that Bruno's system is space- and image-oriented. This is, thus, the very reason why such types of relations are the most popular in his proposition of the semantic field.

of dynamicity has a twofold nature. First of all, Bruno's system is able to generate phrases and sentences due to the fact that the four corners of the square can be assigned different syntactic functions, the concept being moved from corner to corner. Then, remembering that, in a text, a word may be replaced with a metaphor or metonymy, one may thus obtain a different result.

The development of contemporary field theory started at the turn of the 20th century, and was primarily influenced by Humboldt. His doctrine of an *inner speech-form* of language, which reflects the perception of the world and is specific to a certain ethnic group, has provided the basis for all major variants of field theory. However, it was not only Humboldt's doctrine on the relations between language and thinking that had a considerable impact on the rise and development of field theory. The birth of this approach was also stimulated by the advent of Saussurean structuralism, where a lexical field was defined as an organised totality of the elements which define and delimit each other.

It must be mentioned in connection with this that these first doctrines were followed by a number of other, more or less advanced, viewpoints, such as those of Porzig (1928, 1934), Stern (1931), Trier (1931), Jolles (1934), Öhman (1951), Matoré (1951), Ullmann (1957, 1972), Oksaar (1958), Buttler (1967), Perchonock and Werner (1969), Lehrer (1974) and others. However, it is generally agreed that it is Trier's (1931) version of field theory that opened a new era in the history of semantics. Working on the field of INTELLECT in Old and Middle High German periods, the author proposed the notion of the *linguistic field*, which is a section of general vocabulary where the degree of importance of a given individual lexical item is determined by its neighbours. Furthermore, the German scholar claimed that fields are covered by areas of words resembling mosaics, have clear-cut boundaries without any gaps or overlaps, and the change of one component or its deletion within the field automatically results in the change of the whole system. In the words of Trier:

> [t]he accuracy of understanding of an individual word depends on the spiritual presence of the whole context and its particular structure. [...] Words are senseless if the hearer lacks the contrast words from the same conceptual field[3]. (quoted after Buttler 1967: 46; transl. Kleparski and Rusinek 2007a: 76).

One can observe that Trier's (1931) central idea focuses on single elements composing wider and higher circles. For Saussure (1916: 157):

---

3 Die Genauigkeit des Verstehens eines Einzelwortes ist abhängig von der seelischen Gegenwärtigkeit des Gesamtfeldes und seiner besondern Struktur. [...] Worte sind sinnlos, wenn ihre Kontrastworte aus dem gleichen Begriffsfeld dem Hörer fehlen (Buttler 1967: 46).

the idea of value (...) shows that to consider a term as simply the union of a certain sound with a certain concept is grossly misleading. To define it in this way would isolate the term from its system; it would mean assuming that one can start from the terms and construct the system by adding them together when, on the contrary, it is from the interdependent whole that one must start and through analysis obtain its elements.

Therefore, it is evident that the debt which Trier (1931) acknowledges to this French linguist is vast. However, as Gordon (1982: 72) notes, the two scholars differ in certain respects:

Trier finds a specific purpose for such a theory and in this respect he differs clearly from Saussure. (...) Saussure limits himself to presenting his interpretation, whereas Trier proceeds to make practical and detailed application of the theory he has constructed.

Trier's conception of the field amounted to saying that the vocabulary of a synchronic stage of a language, arranged according to principles of content, is organised in *Wortfelder*, or a hierarchical relationship, to one another. The content of the units belonging to the field is determined by mutual delimitation, taking into consideration other neighbouring units. It is interesting to note that Trier did not use the term *semantic field*, but rather *linguistic field*.[4] He stated that:

Fields are linguistic realities existing between single words and the total vocabulary; they are parts of a whole and resemble words in that they resolve themselves into smaller unit[5] (quoted after Coseriu and Geckeler's (1981).

In other words, the part-whole relationship that exists between individual lexemes and the lexical field to which they belong is of the same character as the part-whole relationship that exists between the lexical fields and the whole lexicon.

Trier believed that every language structures the world in a different way, its elements being essential and sufficient to constitute a coherent and comprehensive means of referring to reality. However, the question that arises in connection with this is that of the place of fields in the overall view of language. The answer

---

4   It is necessary to mention in this context that Trier (1931) – apart from singling out the lexical *Wortfelder* – also distinguished conceptual fields, that is *Begriffsfelder*; the latter being equal to the sense of a lexeme (its concept). A lexical field consists of a word and all its conceptually related terms, and a conceptual field is articulated by the lexical field.

5   Felder sind die zwischen den Einzelworten und dem Wortganzen lebendigen sprachlichen Wirklichkeiten, die als Teilganze mit dem Wort das Merkmal gemeinsam haben, dass sie sich ergliedern, mit dem Wortschatz hingegen, dass sie sich ausgliedern[5] (quoted after Ullmann, 1957: 157).

is the following: the field is an integral part of the linguistic whole. Let us give voice to Trier himself:

> We cannot talk of the field without knowing where it is situated within the whole construct of linguistic contents. For it is ultimately aimed at this whole. The field is always something that points beyond itself. Only this makes it a field. (Trier 2008[6]: 42)

Despite its great impact on the development of semantics, Trier's approach has been severely criticised by many scholars for a number of reasons. Firstly, according to Gordon (1982: 70, 72), Trier devoted most of his study only to *Kunst – List – Wisheit*[7] relations. Therefore, it would be a mistake to claim that all other lexical fields bear even a small similarity to the field of INTELLIGENCE as analysed by him. Secondly, not only do many blame him for an unfortunate selection of medieval German texts, since the information about the language of the period under consideration is far from reliable, but also, thirdly, Trier is considered to have employed a variety of terms without a clear explanation of their senses, which apparently renders his analysis even more vague. For instance, in the words of Lyons (1977: 251),

> it is uncertain whether 'area' ('Bezirk') is synonymous with 'field' ('Feld') and how, if at all, 'lexical field' ('Wortfeld') is to be distinguished from 'conceptual field' ('Sinnfeld'). (…) There is the further difficulty that Trier does not explain what he means by 'sense' ('Sinn') and what he means by 'meaning' ('Bedeutung'), and how each of these is to be distinguished from the obviously Saussurean 'value' ('Geltung').

Hence, we need to remember that, while analysing Trier's theory, we must remain vigilant about his terminology.

In addition, Dornseiff (1938: 119–138) points out that the imprecision in defining the analysed concepts can be perceived as a serious blow to field theories, and Oksaar (1958: 15) advises a more individual attitude towards the concept of a given field, for "the vocabulary of each individual is set out differently". This is not, however, the end of the critical viewpoint on Jost Trier. Both Apresjan (1966: 46–47) and Miller (1968) concentrate on the lack in Trier's work of a formal linguistic methodology, maintaining that the scholar's method is only speculative, intuitive and devoid of a serious analysis of linguistic data. Schwarz (1959), along with Coseriu and Geckeler (1981), also claim that Trier did not use any

---

6   The work was published in 1934. 2008 is the publication of the English translation of the article.

7   *Kunst* conveys the knowledge and skills of a courtly knight (e.g. the chivalric code of honour), *List* is the knowledge and skills of those who do not belong to the nobility, and *Wisheit* is a general term for knowledge and skills.

method whatsoever. A similar viewpoint is shared by Geeraerts (2010: 26), who states that

> the descriptive, philological aspect of Trier's study also attracted criticism. Specifically, the texts on which his study is based cannot be considered representative for Old High German and Middle High German in general, as Trier restricted his study of the situation in 1300 to the texts of the mystic Eckehart.

Thus both the quality of Trier's methodology and his selection and choice of data seems dubious.

It has been frequently pointed out that Trier's theory does leave room for either polysemy or homonymy. Furthermore, not only should members of a given lexical field belong to one and the same part of speech, but their meanings are also dependant on both paradigmatic and syntagmatic relations and not solely on the former (Burkhanov 1999: 54–55). Ullmann (1972) also approaches the proposal with strong reservations. There has been severe criticism advanced against the criteria for the exact delimitation of lexical fields due to the fact that such linguistic phenomena as vagueness, synonymy and ambiguity work against it. In the words of Buttler (1967:48),

> Trier treated language as a semiotic system (for instance, a combination of road signs), not taking into account its most essential distinguishing feature, i.e. the ability to create combinations of simple signs. (trans. Żyśko)[8]

Furthermore, it has been pointed out by many that the whole vocabulary of a language can hardly be covered by fields in the same way as fields are covered by words.

However, what seems to be Trier's greatest flaw in the eyes of Oksaar (1958: 42) and Lehrer (1974:17) is the fact that words in a field need not have a clear-cut structure, but some areas of vocabulary tend to overlap or be unsystematic. A similar view comes from Guiraud (1976: 80–81), who claims that:

> The idea of a lexical field, which would be homogenous, without any gaps or overlaps, does not stand up to examination whenever we go beyond the privileged field of intellectual terms, as analysed by Trier: vocabulary related to the physical and material world never has clear-cut boundaries[9]. (trans. Żyśko)

---

8   Trier traktował język jak każdy inny system semiotyczny (np. układ znaków drogowych), nie biorąc pod uwagę jego najistotniejszej cechy odróżniającej: możności tworzenia kombinacji znaków prostych.

9   [s]ama idea pola językowego, które byłoby jednorodne, bez luk, bez zachodzących na siebie fragmentów – nie zdaje egzaminu, gdy wykraczamy poza uprzywilejowaną dziedzinę pojęć intelektualnych, badaną właśnie przez Triera: słownictwo dotyczące fizycznego i materialnego świata nie ma nigdy ostro wytyczonych granic.

We cannot treat a lexical field as a rigid grouping of words, where one item stands next to another without bearing even the slightest resemblance to its neighbours. What is more, Trier (1931) also lays himself open to Geeraerts's (2010) criticism on the same aspect of his theory. The latter scholar maintains that Trier's

> *Lückenlosigkeit* (absence of hiatuses) is contradicted by the existence of lexical gaps, i.e. gaps in the lexical field that occur when a concept – that for reasons of systematicity seems to be a bona fide member of the conceptual field – is not lexicalized.' (Geeraerts 2010: 65)

There have also been criticisms of Trier's proposals that have proved to be wrong. One of these comes form Spence (1961: 92), who having misunderstood Trier, criticises him for allegedly saying that a meaning cannot exist outside a whole field which, together with its neighbours, must be present whenever one wants to comprehend a word. Gordon (1982: 74) defends Trier, stating that the linguist

> does not maintain that the meaning of a term is established exclusively by commutal delimitation. The field establishes the exact extension of a word but the word can be used meaningfully without a knowledge of all its conceptual cognates.[10]

In conclusion, let me say that Trier's impact on the study of word grouping is undoubtedly immense. His vision of a semantic field, although not devoid of imperfections, has made the linguistic community pay attention to the issue of semantically related vocabulary items.

1.3 Post-Trier enthusiasts of semantic fields

The theory of semantic fields started to gain momentum in the 1960s. As a result, field theory was used in a variety of analyses on the quantitative, as well as the qualitative aspects of language. Let us now have a look at the work of Trier's followers.

1.3.1 From Weisgerber to Coseriu

Trier's ideas were followed by Leo Weisgerber (1962), so that now one is justified in speaking about the Trier-Weisgerber field theory. The latter scholar, who based his research on Humboldt's philosophy, while being an enthusiastic adherent of Jost Trier, was aware of his mentor's shortcomings. Contrary to Trier, Weisgerber (1962: 93) believed that language, being a cultural product shaping people's knowl-

---

10 One needs to remember that Trier, despite severe criticism as presented above, is not without his supporters. The greatest of them is Öhman (1953: 123–134), who entirely accepts his theory. She believes that Trier's approach provides a useful methodology for future linguistic study.

edge and understanding of the world, has a substantial influence both on human thought and on the evolution of concepts. Furthermore, he seems to have been right to have drawn a demarcation line between linguistic and logical concepts:

> Linguistic concepts – it concerns these, and only in reference to these is the expression 'concept' correct – are completely distinct from those which are represented by logical concepts. They are, as I have repeatedly pointed out, by no means universally valid, also of the affective type. Their determination in many cases is based upon the principle of mutual delimitation. (Weisgerber, 1962: 93; transl. Żyśko)[11]

The core of Weisgerber's field theory is the *Sprachinhalt* doctrine, together with the *Begriffslehre* (the interdependence of concepts). Contrary to Trier, Weisgerber (1962: 203) offered a method for dealing with the problem of homonymy, an issue very much problematic to field theory. To be more specific, in the eyes of this scholar homonyms are nothing more than separate concepts, which ought not to be mistaken due to their identical forms. Having examined three different semantic fields, such as the semantic fields of NATURAL PHENOMENA, MATERIAL CULTURE and INTELLECT, Weisgerber (1962) claimed that:

> Linguistic field is an extract from the linguistic inter-world which is composed of a whole group of linguistic signs which cooperate with each other in an organic structure (quoted after Coseriu and Geckeler, 1981: 24; transl. Kleparski and Rusinek 2007a: 77)[12]

Such a philosophy, however, comes under attack from Rayevska (1979: 31):

> [The] considerations about the existence of the so-called 'Zwischenwelt', i.e. 'intermediate universe of concepts interposed between man and the universe' lead away from the real essence of language as a means of communication.

In other words, she does not perceive the hypothesis of the inter-world of concepts as going in the right direction. This linguist is supported in her criticism by Ginzburg, Khidekel, Knyazeva and Sankin (1966: 83), who state that language is not quite a go-between for people and reality. In fact, human experience does not differ from one language to another, because we explore the world "not only

---

11 Die sprachlichen Begriffe – um solche handelt es sich und nur in Bezug auf diese ist der Ausdruck ‚Begriff' gerechtfertigt – sind aber recht verschieden von dem was man sich unter logischen Begriff vorstellt. Sie sind, wie ich wiederholt andeutete, durchaus nicht allgemeingültig, sondern sehr start durch subjektive Faktoren, auch gefühlsmässiger Art, bedingt. Ihre Bestimmtheit beruht in vielen Fällen auf dem Prinzip der gegenseitigen Abgrenzung.

12 Ein Sprachliches Feld ist also ein Ausschnitt aus der sprachlichen Zwischenwelt, der durch die Ganzheit einer in organischer Gliederung zusammenwirkenden Gruppe von Sprachzeichen aufgebaut wird.

through linguistic experience, but primarily through our actual contact with the real world". This, therefore, becomes a step towards cognition.

While Trier himself avoided the term *semantic field*, it was freely employed by Porzig (1928, 1934) and Jolles (1934). However, compared to Trier's (1931) original idea, the viewpoints of his followers were relatively modest. It is important to note at this point that it is Ipsen (1924) who used the term *semantic field* for the first time in the history of linguistics. He focused on a set of words joined by overt morphological and semantic indicators, looking at the field of Indo-European terms associated with the field of METALS. Searching for the criteria for the existence of fields, the author stated that they are rooted in the formal and functional assimilation of their components. What is more, according to his theory the framework of the field, as well as the relationship between its components, remain unaltered despite their change and replacement by synonyms. Trier (1934) criticised such a viewpoint and maintained that such a field concept could work only while analysing remote periods of Indo-European languages.

For Jolles (1934), on the other hand, semantic fields were minimal fields consisting of two members only, e.g. *Vater – Sohn, Tag – Nacht*, etc. For many, including Coseriu and Geckeler (1981), this approach to the concept of the field did not greatly contribute to the evolution of field theory, many valuable observations notwithstanding.

In the meantime, Saussure turned out to be the cornerstone of another language system analysis. Bally (1940), acknowledging his debts to the Swiss linguist, drew on the principle of structuralism in order to apply it to the associative field theory. He described each word as "the centre of a constellation, the point where an indefinite number of other coordinated terms converge" (quoted after Ullmann 1972: 368). The so-called associative relations, linked together due to the presence of a common root-element, or due to their relatedness of meaning, are exemplified in the following manner:

Fig. 2. Associative relations according to Bally (1940).

read <> reader <> reading <> readable <> reread
reading <> book <> page <> letter <> education

It must be mentioned at this point that – in an era of little interest in historical semantics – Bally (1940) claimed that the associations might influence the semantic development of words.

Another linguist who contributed to the development of field theory was Öhman (1951). Her interests focus mainly on the same semantic fields in several modern languages, aiming to show the dependence of reality on the peculiarities of a given language. Let us give an example of two lexical items belonging to two languages of the same language family, that is, English and German.[13]

Fig. 3. *The difference between English* highschool *and German* Hochschule.

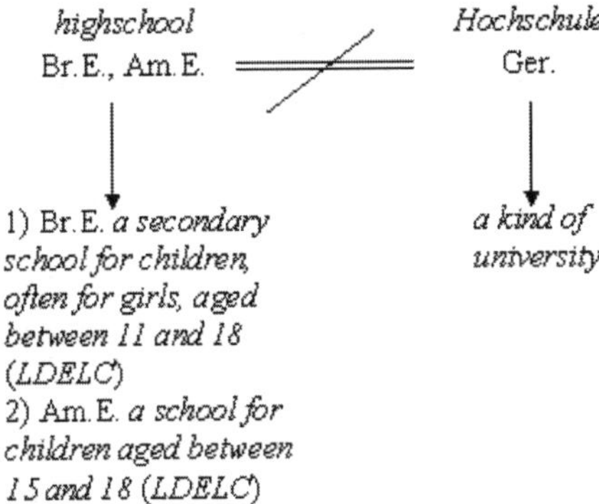

Another linguist, Coseriu (1967), having investigated lexical fields and their sensitivity to language variability, i.e. dialect differences, proposed the following definition of *Wortfeld*:

> From a structural point of view, a lexical field (Wortfeld) is a lexical paradigm constituted by different words of a language that are directly opposed to one another by simple content-distinguishing features and that jointly subdivide a lexical continuum of content (quoted after Lieb 1978: 66–67).

1.3.2 Porzig's intrinsic meaning relations

It seems reasonable to claim that, out of the aforementioned linguists, it is Porzig (2008)[14] whose theory deserves closest attention. The author concentrates on the syntagmatic relations of lexical items, where the use of one determines the appearance of another. According to the author, the core of such a relationship is either a verb or an adjective, e.g. *ride – a camel, bark – a dog, blond – hair*, etc. In his view, such word pairs form semantic fields, for

---

13 Interestingly, the German term *Hochschule* is the equivalent of Polish *Szkoła Wyższa*, being an institute of higher education.

14 The work was originally published in 1934. 2008 is the publication of the English translation of the article.

[j]ust as *walking* requires *feet, grasping* requires a *hand, seeing* requires *eyes, hearing* requires *ears, licking* requires a *tongue* and *kissing* requires *lips*. This is (…) a semantic relation that is grounded in the nature of the meanings themselves. For this reason, I shall call these relations intrinsic meaning relations. (Porzig 2008: 3)

Therefore, as Porzig (2008: 4) notes,

[t]he most basic relation that a semantic field can have is evidently the relation that holds between two words. Because of this, intrinsic meaning relations, as defined above, can also be called elementary semantic fields.

Thus, it is the meaning of the word that binds it tightly to other words and, consequently, it is at the core of lexical relations. Moreover, it is necessary to mention that the notion of the (elementary) semantic field is not the only one introduced by Porzig. The scholar was convinced that the group of words associated with the centre of the field stands for a paratactic field, e.g.

Fig. 4. An example of Porzig's paratactic field.

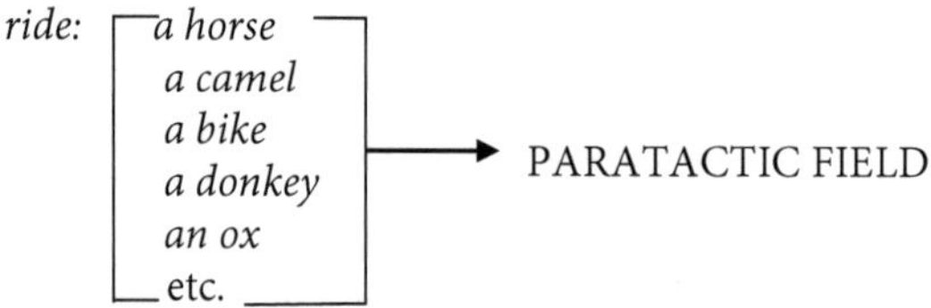

At the same time, paratactic fields contain words which are also located in a syntactic field, e.g.:

Fig. 5. Examples of Porzig's syntactic fields.

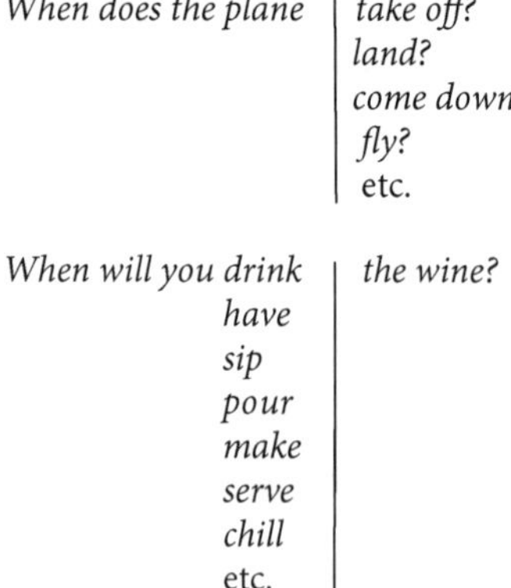

Furthermore, Porzig proposes a two-way insight into the notion of the semantic field, i.e. the synchronic and diachronic one. Therefore, having looked at the theory from a synchronic perspective, the linguist comes to the straightforward conclusion that

> the existence of etymological relations does not guarantee the existence of an intrinsic meaning relation. Although only a *Richter* 'judge' can *richten* 'pronounce a judgement' it is not true that only a *writer* can 'write' [.] (Porzig 2008: 10)

Thus, as we can deduce from the above quotation, etymologically linked word groups do not necessarily equal semantically linked word groups. As a result, one is right to state that etymological groups and semantic fields are independent, although not mutually exclusive.

However, taking into consideration the diachronic perspective, Porzig (2008) presupposes a constant alteration and flexibility of fields, which is the most essential difference between his and Trier's (1931) theory of fields. As the author mentions, "[n]ew intrinsic meaning relations emerge continuously, they emerge from the inevitable conditions of social life[.]" (Porzig 2008: 20).

However, a degree of criticism of Porzig's theory is in order. In the words of Gordon (1982: 88), Porzig's (1928, 1934) elementary semantic relations are, in fact, collocations of words in their literal meaning; e.g. Porzig's own example is that of the verb *to grasp*, which presupposes the noun *hand*. To be more specific, the linguist maintains that as soon as the verb is used at the metaphorical level, e.g. in the sentence *I grasp your meaning*, the implicit hand is no longer essential in the relation. Gordon (1982: 88), following Trier (1934), criticises this one-way word relation, for, according to him,

> [t]he serious flaw in Porzig's theory, therefore, is that the elementary semantic relations which he postulates are not even reciprocal. When he tells us that "to grasp" presupposes "the hand" he neglects the fact that the reverse case is not necessarily true. A semantic relation which fails to meet so basic a requirement is of little merit.

According to Trier (1934), this is the greatest drawback to Porzig's approach to language, and the former's critical view of the proposal is clearly expressed in just one sentence:

> One can see now that Porzig's field cannot be compared with Ipsen's. Both are fundamentally distinct and have only this one thing in common, that neither of them resemble Trier's. (Trier, 1934: 439) [15]

---

15 Man sieht nun, dass das Porzigsche Feld mit dem Ipsenschen nicht gleichgesetzt werden kann. Die beiden sind grundverschieden und haben nur dies eine gemeinsam, dass keins von ihnen dem Trierschen gleicht.

Thus, neither Porzig's nor Ipsen's approaches bear any resemblance in their proposals to Trier's linguistic philosophy, which can imply that none of them can even approximate it in terms of quality. If we take the 'hand-words' analysed by him as an instance of a semantic field, it seems doubtful whether all verbs presupposing 'the hand', without being conceptually related to one another (such as *write*, *punch*, *grasp*, *push*, or *lift*), could be included in it.

The next factor against the application of Porzig's theory is the fact that the linguist, working on people's particular utterances, failed to mark the line of distinction between the existing word relations. With reference to this, Buttler (1967: 52) claims that:

> The hypothesis of the overlapping of syntactic and paratactic fields is open to doubt; not all words existing in the same 'place' of a syntactic field form a coherent semantic group. (transl. Kleparski and Rusinek (2007a: 78)[16]

Porzig's (1928, 1934) viewpoint seems to be the basis for Oksaar's (1958) hypothesis, according to which semantic fields both intermingle and overlap. However, it must be pointed out that the basic unit of the latter scholar's analysis is not a field but rather a word – an autonomic element. Therefore, Oksaar pays particular attention to the role of stylistic and word-formation factors, which are likely to have a great impact on the organisation of fields falling into sets of specialised, colloquial or ornamental expressions.

1.3.3 Mot-témoin *vs.* mot-clé

Many viewpoints have been issued on field theory so far, however neither Trier nor his followers bothered to explain the reasons for this phenomenon. Therefore, it seems fair to say that Matoré (1953: 66), to whom we owe the notions of *mot-témoin* (witness word) and *mot-clé* (key word), takes a step forward, trying to seek the rationale for sense shifts in the evolution of social structures and institutions. To quote the lexicologist:

> The witness-word is the symbol of a change. It is a neologism; the sudden change which gives rise to it is the sign of a new social, economic or aesthetic situation. It marks a turning point. (Matoré, 1953: 66; transl. Żyśko) [17]

---

16 Wątpliwość budzi też zasada przecinania się pól syntaktycznych i parataktycznych; nie wszystkie wyrazy występujące w tym samym 'miejscu' pola syntaktycznego tworzą spoistą grupę znaczeniową. (Buttler 1967: 52).

17 Le mot-témoin est le symbole d'un <u>changement</u> (…) Le mot-témoin est un néologisme; la mutation brusque qui lui donne naissance est le signe d'une nouvelle situation sociale

Therefore, as we can deduce from the quotation above, Matoré's method of analysing word groupings tends to have a paralinguistic character, since he takes the view that, on the strength of analysing vocabulary, we are in a position to explain the society that uses it. Thus, when it comes to the grouping of words, Matoré (1953) emphasises that what needs to be taken into consideration and treated as the only factor of membership in a group is purely the social value of a word. Consequently, it is the social relevance which dictates the hierarchy in the lexicon. This is how words not necessarily conceptually linked to each other are placed within the same field, the dominant unit being the *mot-clé*: expressing order in the lexicon, it designates an idea or a feeling currently recognised by the society as its ideal.

For many linguists, Matoré (1953), although proposing a paralinguistic way of treating semantic fields, does not depart very far in his ideas from Trier (1931) himself. In the words of Guiraud (1976: 84), the two scholars differ in terms of their viewpoints on semantic fields, and the methodological apparatus:

> It is only a matter of temperament and the point of view – not to mention the method – which differentiates Matoré from Trier. This one is a 'philosopher' and belongs to the German tradition of the idealistic school; that one is a 'sociologist' from the French school, to which such linguists as Meillet, Brunot, Vendryes belong. Trier, above all, examines the spiritual and ethical life in order to capture 'the spirit' of a given nation and a given epoch, whereas Matoré is occupied mainly with the material, economic, technical and political background of lexis. (Guiraud 1976: 84; transl. Żyśko) [18]

Matoré was aware of Trier's (1931) merits as well as shortcomings. Thus, the French linguist did not hesitate to diverge from the father of field theory. Firstly, his subject of analysis was a modern language. Secondly, we can deduce from his work that, according to him, Trier should have limited his research to a precisely established period of time.

Nevertheless, irrespective of all his contributions to the study of semantic fields, Matoré (1953) does attract some critical views. To mention a few, Gordon (1982: 130) doubts whether drawing a demarcation line between semantics and lexicology

---

économique, esthétique, etc. (…) il marquee un <u>tournant</u>. (Matoré, 1953: 66; emphasis original).

18 To tylko kwestia temperamentu i punktu widzenia – by nie wspomnieć o metodzie – dzieli Matorégo od Triera. Tamten jest „filozofem" i należy do tradycji niemieckiej szkoły idealistycznej; ten jest „socjologiem" ze szkoły francuskiej do której należą tacy językoznawcy jak Meillet, Brunot, Vendryes. Trier bada przede wszystkim życie duchowe i etyczne gwoli uchwycenia „ducha" danego narodu i danej epoki, podczas gdy Matoré zajmuje się głównie materialnym, ekonomicznym, technicznym i politycznym podłożem leksyki. Guiraud (1976: 84).

is given enough justification. Theory and method do not seem to be distinguished, either, which could be perceived as a grave mistake. Last but not least, correlating the linguistic and sociological data appears to be a little troublesome, since this implies that cause and effect are not distinguished from each other.

1.3.4 The field structure of life

In 1936, Kurt Lewin (1936) claimed that not only language, but also human life has a field structure. Therefore, as he maintains, a person's life-space has two aspects. Firstly, an individual should be regarded as an integral part of a life-space. Every person with their inner area is treated as an intrapersonal domain. Secondly, all paths in the life-space along with their life obstacles are treated as locomotion (Wildgen 2000). But what is the function of language in such a structure? First of all, language transfers a person's internal states to his or her environment. In addition, it enables indirect locomotion in the psychological space. Original as Lewin's ideas are, they did not manage to acquire sufficient interest and do not have followers in field semantics.

1.4 Later trends in field theory

Bearing the foregoing remarks in mind, let us remind ourselves that the growing popularity of cognitive linguistic analyses brought a breath of fresh energy and ideas to the study of language and semantic fields. It is definitely beneficial for any theory to be supplemented and enriched with ideas from other disciplines – which is precisely what happened to field theory, which, over the course of time, gained more momentum thanks to arguments of a conceptual nature.

1.4.1 The nature of field boundaries

Perchonock and Werner (1969: 229–242), working on terms associated with the field FOOD in Navaho, gave evidence for a variety of relations within the lexicon. A similar view was formulated by Lehrer (1974:18):

> I have found that speakers disagree among themselves, and often have difficulty in deciding whether two words overlap in meaning or contrast, and whether one term is included in the meaning of another.

Note that the author seems to be greatly influenced by the work of Berlin and Kay (1969: 1–23), which has come to serve as the fundamental issue in cognitive semantics. The study of the field of COLOUR led the authors to the conclusion that the boundaries between fields (colour categories) are fuzzy, while the most typical examples of their components are focal points. Furthermore, the authors present a hypothesis concerning a maximal set of eleven perceptual foci of colours and the order in which they are acquired by children, as shown below in Fig. 6.

Fig. 6. Berlin and Kay's (1969) stages of acquisition of terms of COLOUR.

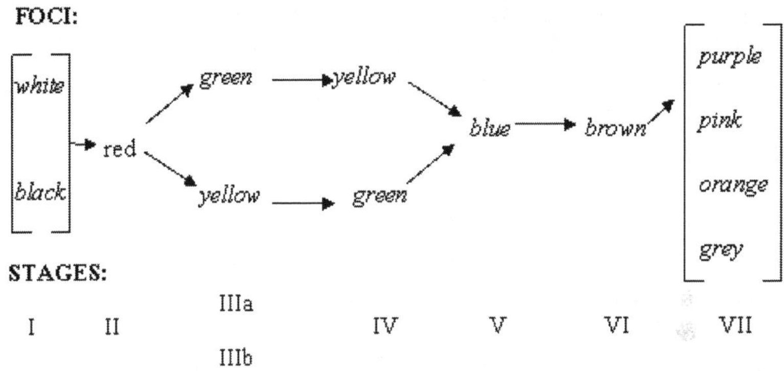

This was a very seminal study, one that has been widely accepted worldwide to the extent that today it seems impossible to imagine field boundaries as clear-cut, the fields resembling mosaics, without gaps or overlaps. Alongside Berlin and Kay, the viewpoint concerning fuzzy boundaries and basic terms has been eagerly accepted. Thus, the fuzziness of boundaries is the standard view these days. Quoting Tokarski (1993: 355),

> The justification for such a fuzziness of field boundaries is also to be sought in the lexical semantic properties. Within almost all analysed fields (probably except for closed classes such as 'days of the week', 'seasons') some vocabulary items constitute the centre of the field, are quickly associated with it, and their reconstruction is not a great deal of trouble. The further one gets from the centre, the bigger the problems with delineating the boundary and lexical composition of the field are. (transl. Żyśko) [19]

One can say on the basis of this that a semantic field can be compared to a dissipating halo radiating form the centre. Thus, it is evident that the items that belong to the core of the halo are the most characteristic of the whole structure.

---

19 [t]aka rozmytość granic pola ma również uzasadnienie w znaczeniowych właściwościach leksyki. W obrębie niemal wszystkich analizowanych pól (z wyjątkiem może klas zamkniętych typu „dni tygodnia", „pory roku") pewna część słownictwa stanowi centrum tego pola, jest z nim kojarzona najszybciej i jej odtworzenie nie stanowi poważniejszego problemu. Im dalej od centrum, tym kłopoty z wyznaczeniem precyzyjnej granicy i składu leksykalnego pola są większe. (Tokarski 1993: 355).

The rise of cognitive linguistics caused more criticism of the structuralist theory of fields, and not only of its idea of clear-cut field boundaries. Sweetser (1990: 25), criticising semantic field theory for the fact that "semantic-field analyses cannot explain why polysemy and semantic change frequently cross between fields – for example, why (…) *see* and *know* should be related concepts", explains the reason for her criticism. This is to be found in the linguist's postulates presupposing metaphorisation as the key explanation of the relationship between senses. Metaphors connect vocabulary items of originally distant domains, leading to the overlap of their meanings. At the same time, Sweetser (1990) becomes one more scholar rejecting the strictness of field boundaries.

1.4.2 The issue of membership in a semantic field

Lehrer (1974: 10) realises that "not all items in a field are of equal status, and it is useful to distinguish between basic and peripheral words". The linguist would seem to be right in maintaining that a word that is peripheral in one field can be a central member of another related category (1974: 12). Thus, an item's membership in a field is delimited by the following criteria (Lipka 1980: 98–99):

a) the members of a field must be in direct opposition in the same syntactic hole; to understand this properly, membership in a field means being in the same word-class. In the case of semantic fields with modifier plus head components, it is the syntactic class of the head that decides on the membership of the unit. Thus, transitive and intransitive verbs, for instance, do not belong to the same field.

b) the members of a field must have at least one specific semantic component/ feature in common. See Rusinek (2008b) and Kleparski and Rusinek (2008), whose research has shown that *Zouave* and *shawl* have had a common feature in their semantic evolutions.

c) "field membership must be established due to objective procedures" indispensable while delimiting and structuring lexical fields, the former being dealt with externally and internally as well. The external delimitation of a field, usually associated with its extension, is marked by the presence or absence of an archilexeme and a common set of features. The internal one, on the other hand, is fraught with more difficulties, for not only are idiolect and other language variations apt to be troublesome, but the central and peripheral position of an item in a field should also be considered.

As for the common features the members of a field should possess, these can be:

a) distinctive – these are the most essential components, since their task is to distinguish lexical items; thus, they usually function in opposition;
b) connotative – these features are also an inherent part of the lexeme; it is their presence or absence that distinguishes items from one another, e.g. *horse* from *steed*;
c) inferential – the features appear in context and are not inherent, e.g. (no work) in the case of the item 'holiday';
d) relational – as in the previous case, they are essential for dealing with syntagmatic relations; they help to differentiate two relative items, for instance *father* and *son*;
e) transfer – as Lipka (1980: 112) mentions, these components "may be used to capture metaphorical processes", e.g. "the verb *drink* contains a feature <-Solid> transferred to its object";
f) deictic – these have the character of distinctive components, since they explain oppositions, as in the case of *now* and *then*, *push* and *pull*.

However, the question that arises in connection with this is how one recognises whether a certain lexical item actually belongs to a given semantic field. To answer this, it is important to consider linear, i.e. non-hierarchic fields, and hierarchic fields separately. As far as a linear field is concerned, Lipka (1990: 152) goes on to state that criterion b) of its definition equals the statement that the field covers a whole 'dimension', for instance, age, temperature, sex, etc. These, on the other hand, can be binary and non-binary in type. It should be mentioned here that the classification of a non-binary contrast, as proposed by Lyons (1977: 289) and Leech (1981: 100), mentions scales, cycles and multiple taxonomy. A scale involves gradual opposition, as the members of the field are gradable, e.g. *colder*, *warmer*. An example of a linear field based on a scale is one whose members have the semantic component 'temperature' in common:

Fig. 7. The linear field of temperature in the form of a scale (after Lipka 1990: 152).

$$\longleftarrow \quad 0 \quad \longrightarrow$$

hot	warm	tepid	cool	cold

According to Lipka (1990: 153), another type of a linear field is the cycle, as best exemplified by colour terms:

Fig. 8. The linear field of colour in the form of a cycle (after Lipka 1990: 153).

red	yellow	green	blue	purple

As he mentions, "[n]o single element in the chain of oppositions is above any other, nor does it show a greater degree of some quality. The items all have the same status" (Lipka 1990: 153). Therefore, it seems evident that the members of the field concerned form a cycle.

The third type of linear field appears to have been widely accepted from Leech (1981: 100). The so called "multiple taxonomy" involves non-gradable items which cannot be opposed to one another in the way *stallion* is to *mare*, i.e. 'male horse' vs. 'female horse'. Thus, these fields are not restricted to adjectives, incorporating, according to Leech, nouns of such common semantic components as metal, breed, species, kind, etc.

When it comes to hierarchic fields, the method of field-study as proposed by Cruse (1975: 28) and Lyons (1977: 292) provides a test for hyponymy:

A(n) X is a kind of Y

For instance, as put forward by the latter,

(1) A *cow* is an animal of *a certain kind*.
(2) To *buy* something is to get something in *a certain way*.

where the italicised fragment at the end of the structure remains unspecified.

Lipka (1980: 100–101), however, in order to capture the specific kind of relation between field members and, consequently, discover and justify its semantic components, goes beyond the above hyponymy test, and proposes his own test-formula as the basis for a paraphrase evaluation:

$$X \text{ is(t) ein / a (\quad) } Y$$

It should be noted that the modifier in parentheses is equivalent to Lyons' and Cruse's 'in a certain way', and the semantic components can be established provided that X can be replaced by a modifier plus head in the same syntactic position. To support the above hypotheses, let me introduce the English version of Lipka's (1980: 101) example:

(3) The man *ran* down the street.
(4) The man *went* (quickly) down the street.

Therefore, following Baumgärtner's (1967: 165–197) method of drawing a diagram for the field represented by the archilexeme *sterben*, Lipka (1980: 103–105) goes on to propose his own representation of the archilexeme *strike*, a microfield within the macro-field of contact verbs. However, by introducing certain modifications, i.e. Lehrer's (1974: 84) marking of optional components by braces and the specification of obligatory features in square brackets, as well as using capitals for general categories, Lipka (1980: 104) slightly changes Baumgärtner's (1967) ideas, as represented in Fig. 9.

Fig. 9. The field of strike *in a tree diagram (after Lipka 1980).*

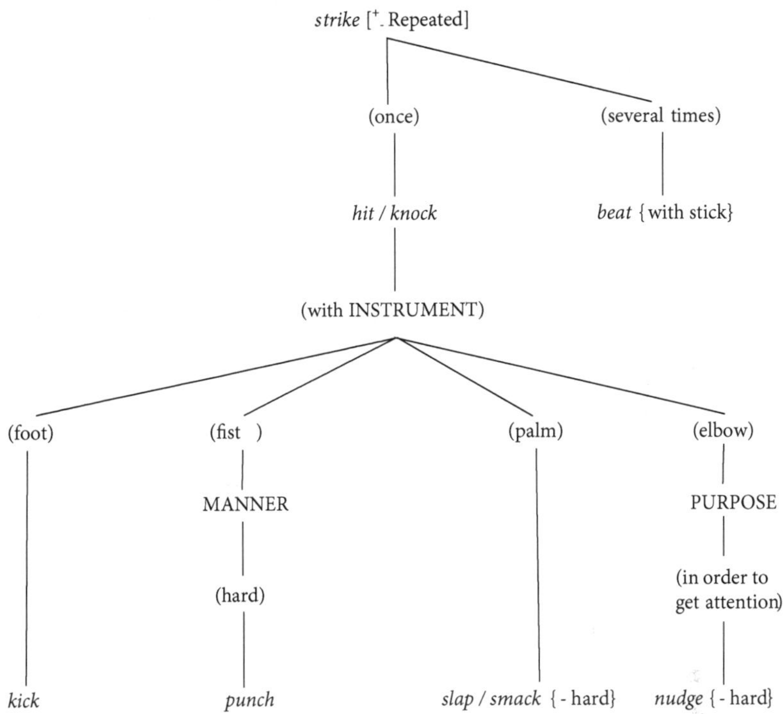

1.4.3 In search of the centre of a semantic field

As has been already noted, the similarity of lexical items belonging to the same semantic field is of crucial importance. Bally (1940) highlights a common root-element, whereas Lipka (1980: 98–99) focuses on a common semantic component/feature. According to another scholar whose major preoccupation is the development of field theory, Jürgen Strauß (1986: 137), the centre of the field is called the field core: this is where basic lexemes are located, i.e. those that are characterised by a common semantic feature. Similar to Ginzburg, Khidekel, Knyazeva and Sankin (1966: 83), Strauß makes it clear that although individual experience may differ depending on one's sex, race, culture, religion, etc., we do generally tend to reach a consensus on the determination of the field core. The reason for this is that "basic terms of a field are lexicalizations of a relatively wide range of conceptual aspects which we, according to our experience, recognize as essential" (Strauß 1986: 137).

However, non-basic terms lexicalise only some of the conceptual aspects associated with the field. These non-basic terms are usually metaphors, metonymies, loan-words, neologisms, etc. Since these, from the viewpoint of cognitive linguists, are the products of conceptualisation, Strauß offers a cognitive/conceptual approach to field semantics. The author explains how the non-basic terms actually influence a semantic field. In the case of a lack of a particular term for an object in a language, a foreign word is borrowed, which results in the filling of lexical gaps. Furthermore, newly coined words can replace already existing ones.

All things considered, and taking into account the fact that all of the above changes within the conceptual field lead to changes in semantic fields, one has good grounds to say that Strauß (1986: 135–144), offering a conceptual approach to field semantics, emphasises the motivating factors lying behind changes in semantic fields. But in order to address the question of what makes terms basic, and how one can recognise them, let me refer to Berlin and Kay (1969: 6–7). The authors, working on basic colour terms, propose eight criteria to distinguish them. Since two of them are restricted to the domain of colour, I will present the remaining six:

1) basic words are monolexemic;
2) the application of a basic term cannot be restricted to a narrow class of objects;
3) the sense of a basic word is not included in the sense of any other word except for the name of the field;
4) a basic word is psychologically salient for informants;
5) doubtful forms ought to have the same distributional potential as the basic words;
6) recent foreign borrowings should be treated suspiciously.

Having investigated the issue of the core of the semantic field, the question that arises in connection with this is one of lexical gaps within a semantic field. Let me briefly discuss this issue in the following section.

1.4.4 Do lexical gaps exist?

The issue of lexical gaps is of crucial importance while analysing the notion of semantic field. Traugott and Dasher (2004: 66) devote some attention to Trier's analysis of lexical fields in the form of mosaics, but it is Lehrer (1974: 95–109, 1977: 95–123) who explores the issue in depth. She distinguishes between four major types of lexical gaps. The first of these are morpheme gaps: possible sequences of segments allowed by phonological rules but non-existent in a given language. Only after a word is borrowed from a foreign language do people realize the gap. Once the word becomes assimilated, the morpheme structure rules alter and the gap is filled.

The second type of lexical gap is the paradigm gap, which Lehrer (1974: 95–96) exemplifies with singular and plural nouns, as seen below:

Fig. 10. An example of a paradigm gap (after Lehrer 1974: 95–96).

SINGULAR	PLURAL
cup	*cups*
dress	*dresses*
–	*trousers*
chaos	–

The next type she proposes is the derivational gap. In her words,

> [d]erivational gaps are produced by putting together partially productive stems and affixes in ordinary ways, with results that are unacceptable, though perfectly comprehensible. Examples of such gaps are *ungood, *mistelephone, *conversate, *insilent,* and *propelment.* (Lehrer 1974: 96)

As we can rightly deduce from the quotation, the gaps concerned can be produced any time we add a productive affix to a lexical item in such a way that the resulting word is ungrammatical. The next type, the matrix gap, becomes visible when related lexical items are analysed in terms of their semantic features and placed on a chart. The suggested example is one concerning verbs that denote the care that one takes of young people, animals and plants, respectively:

Fig. 11. An example of the matrix gap (Lehrer 1974: 97).

	HUMAN	ANIMAL	PLANT
		raise	
make grow	*rear*	–	*grow*

However, no matter how many types of lexical gaps there are, a potential language user is aware of only one type, i.e. the functional one. Such an awareness is raised by the lack of a suitable word that could express the speakers' thoughts.

The existence of lexical gaps is nothing surprising. I do believe that, even if a speaker has no knowledge of the first four types of lexical gap, he/she has probably experienced the problem of functional gaps. In fact, no one knows all lexical items in their own language; we also often experience the "tip-of-the-tongue" phenomenon. The question that rises in connection with this is: once a gap occurs, what happens with it? Lehrer (1974: 106–107) notices that even if there is no appropriate word to express a concept, people tend to use a similar word from the same lexical field. Therefore, she questions the notion of lexical gaps as such:

> Is it really the case that there are lexical gaps that are being filled in by another word in
> the same field, or is the conceptual field divided up like a mosaic, as Trier assumed, so
> that each word covers a wide range of meaning? I think that the answer lies somewhere
> in between, though the correct analysis may differ according to the case. There do seem
> to be genuine gaps, but they can frequently be filled by other words in the lexical field
> because the less important components can be dispensed with. (Lehrer 1974: 106–107)

Lipka (1980: 105), in turn, analyses the hierarchical fields of the English *horse* and the German *Pferd*, for, according to him, "the comparison of fields across languages is in [Lipka's] opinion one of the most fruitful results of field theory". Contrary to English *filly* and *colt*, German *Fohlen* and *Füllen* are not specified for sex. Thus, the German word field is characterised by two gaps (Lipka 1980: 105–107).

Lipka (1980: 108–111) also offers a graphic representation of semantic fields in the form of a diagram and a matrix, the former having the shape of boxes, trees and circles. While box diagrams seem to be perfect for simple representations of hierarchical and linear fields, tree diagrams tend to be employed to reveal the hierarchical structure of a field. Thanks to the fact that these can be labelled or unlabelled, and allow a clear arrangement of lexemes, tree representations of a semantic field have a didactic character. When it comes to circular/radial diagrams, their principal task is to demonstrate the distinction between the centre and the periphery of a field. Matrices, on the other hand, can be employed to elaborate on the structure of both hierarchical fields and those that lack such an ordering. Thus, one has good grounds to state that a matrix tends to be more advantageous than a diagram, as it allows us to present a great deal of details, such as sex, shape, colour, age, etc.

1.4.5 The systematisation of field terminology

Further development in semantic research brought forth Lyons's (1977) classic work on the issue concerned. Assuming that field theory is connected with the analysis of sense, he distinguishes, which Trier (1931) failed to do, the conceptual field, the lexical field, and the semantic field, a lexeme denoting both morpho-logically simple and complex lexical items:

> Lexemes and other units[20] that are semantically related, whether paradigmatically or syntagmatically, within a given language-system can be said to belong to (...) the same (semantic) field; and a field whose members are lexemes is a lexical field. A lexical field is therefore a paradigmatically and syntagmatically structured subset of the vocabulary. (Lyons 1977: 268)

In other words, the lexical field constitutes only a part of the semantic field, which is illustrated in Fig. 12, Lipka's (1980: 94) tree-diagram representation of Lyons's (1977: 253–254) idea of the field, showing its additional binary features:

Fig. 12. The hierarchical structure and semantic content of Lyons's (1977) fields.

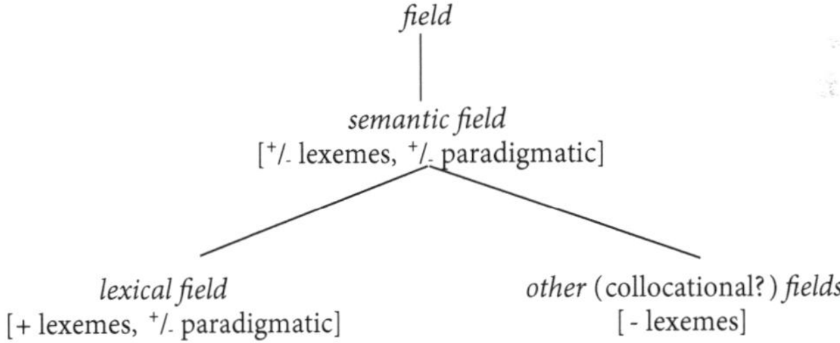

The structure of a lexical field at a given time (t_1) can be compared to the structure of a lexical field at any other time (t_2), since they cover the same conceptual field. Furthermore, the sense of the lexeme is a conceptual area within a conceptual field. In the words of Kleparski and Rusinek (2007b: 194), "the author [Lyons] attributes considerable importance to the concept of context, stating that there is a great deal of syntagmatic and paradigmatic relationships within semantic fields[.]"

All the above approaches to field semantics prompted Lipka (1980) to elaborate on his own interpretation of the issue, criticising the early theories of field semantics. This is because on many occasions, starting with Trier himself, the same terms were used to denote different notions. Such an inconsistency in terminology became a rationale for Lipka (1980: 97) to systematise the concept of field, where B stands for Baumgärnter, C for Coseriu, L for Lyons and Li for Lipka:

semantic field $_L$ = SEMANTIC FIELD $_{Li}$ = Bedeutungsfeld $_B$
lexical field $_L$ ≠ LEXICAL FIELD $_{Li}$ ≠ lexical field $_C$ (= Wortfeld $_C$)

---

20 As Lipka (1980: 93) notes, other units can come, for instance, in the form of collocations.

lexical field $_C$ = WORD-FIELD $_{Li}$ = champ lexical $_C$ (= Wortfeld $_C$)
superordinate lexeme $_L$ = ARCHILEXEME $_{Li}$ = Archilexeme $_C$

It is worth remembering that Lipka's field is apt to show a hierarchical nature, ranging from any modifier plus head to such compounds as idiomatic expressions (1980: 97): modifier / head – familiar collocation – fixed collocation – compound – idiom, which, in a more technical way, can be represented as:

linear field – semantic field – lexical field – word field.

Having introduced such a classification of fields, Lipka then goes on to draw a distinction between them, as can be seen in Table 1:

Table 1. The distinction between fields depending on the use of simple or complex lexemes.

features lexemes / collocations	paradigmatic	lexemes	simple	homogeneous
field	+	o	o	o
semantic field	+	-	o	o
lexical field	+	+	o	o
word-field	+	+	+	+
linear hierarchical field	+	o	o	o

While all types of fields tend to be defined as paradigmatic structures, it is the distinction between lexical field and word field that accounts for the establishment of lexical gaps. These, however, can only exist on the level of "the primary vocabulary, i.e. simple lexical items, if one considers word-formation as a productive process" (Lipka 1980: 98), for "[i]f complex lexemes are admitted in such a field, the productive word-formation processes may close such a gap at any time" (Lipka 1990: 152).

1.5 The diachronic study of meaning: the notion of semantic change

Beginning with Aristotle, through 19th century linguistics and finishing with early 21st century scholarship, the issue of meaning change has always attracted attention. The major question linguists have tried to answer was whether there were any rules or tendencies in developing new meanings. In 1900, Michel Bréal came to the conclusion that there must be some law of specialisation, which would explain the number of specialised functions of a given lexical item. Soon with the arrival of structuralism, studies were conducted with an attempt to consider individual words in isolation. One important contribution to this approach was Jost Trier's (1934) field theory. In order to see the nature of diachronic semantics, let us quote Traugott and Dasher's (2004: 60) reference to Saussure:

> [c]hange emphasizes the arbitrariness of language because individual signs are the result of individual changes over time (even though there may be overall regularities such as the exceptionlessness of sound change). According to Saussure (1996 [1916]: 92), "[i]n spite of appearances to the contrary, diachronic events are always accidental and particular in nature" and not subject to "laws" in the sense of generalizations that are "imperative" and "general" (ibid. p. 90).

What we can infer from this quote is the fact that diachronic semantics is the study of meaning change, apparently interested in the causes of meaning change, but *describing* those changes rather than *explaining* them. As a result, diachronic semantics concentrates on a pure description of what is happening in language, not in the human mind.

One of the most fundamental definitions of semantic change from the diachronic perspective was produced by Stern (1931:163):

> I define change of meaning as the habitual modification, among a comparatively large number of speakers, of the traditional semantic range of the word, which results form the use of the word (1) to denote one or more referents which it has not previously denoted, or (2) to express a novel manner of apprehending one of its referents.

The author considers two viewpoints on sense shifts, namely semasiology – a change of meaning (when a word starts to be used to express a new meaning), as well as onomasiology – a change of name (when a meaning begins to be associated with a new form). Stern also discussed the difference between sense change and sense fluctuation, the former being part of a habitual process, the latter being a matter of individuals.

Ullmann (1957), on the other hand, focuses on the functional aspects of sense alterations. He says:

> If meaning is conceived as a reciprocal relationship obtaining between name and sense, then a semantic change will occur whenever a new name becomes attached to a sense and/or a new sense to name.

Ullmann is conscious of the fact that meaning changes may differ in degrees of complexity, and can be simple or multiple. Another linguist from the second half of the 20th century, Waldron (1967), apart from distinguishing causes of meaning change, recognises certain types of this phenomenon. He understands change of meaning as an alteration in the reference category. Thus, he calls modification within the existing linguistic category a "shift", whereas a change to a different category is a "transfer".

1.5.1 Semantic change: typologies

Within the diachronic study of meaning, a few major types of classification of meaning change can be distinguished: logico-rhetorical, genetic, axiological, empirical and functional.

The author of the logico-rhetorical classification is Paul (1880). The major principle in this typology is the relation between primary and secondary meaning. Thus, on the logico-rhetorical grounds, four main categories of meaning change have been established:

1. Narrowing of meaning – restriction of the meaning of words which were used in a general sense, and with time begin to be used with a specific meaning. Words may narrow their senses as a result of being used by a given social group, as euphemisms, or technical terms, etc., e.g. OE *meta* 'food' changed into ModE *meat* 'the flesh of animals used for food'.
2. Widening of meaning – extension of the senses of words which were formerly used under special conditions, and now start being generalised, e.g. OE *brid* 'a young bird' changed to ModE *bird* 'any creature with wings, feathers that lays eggs and can usually fly'.
3. Transfer of meaning – resulting in the neutralisation of meaning; it is a change of meaning which is potentially implicit in a word with the development of a synonymous meaning, where a word from one semantic field changes into a word belonging to another semantic field, e.g. OE *feoh* 'live-stock' changed to ModE *fee* 'money'.
4. Other changes, which include amelioration and pejoration, as is discussed below.

Another class of typologies of meaning change is the causal one, introduced by Meillet (1921); it is also called genetic classification. The focus of Meillet's research are the causes of semantic changes:

1. Changes caused by modifications in the linguistic signifier, e.g. the French use of the negatives *pas, personne, rien, jamais* on syntagmatic grounds.
2. Changes due to historical reasons caused by changes in the referent, e.g. the products of material culture such as *ship, lamp, torch, pen, coach*, etc.,
3. Changes due to social stratification caused by the specialisation of the meaning of words, e.g. Lat. *ponere* 'to put' changed to Fr. *ponder* 'to lay eggs'.

Stern (1931) develops an empirical classification of meaning alterations:

1. Substitution, which is a sense change due to non-linguistic causes. The basic reason for this alteration is the fact that referents change and people require new names for them.

The constant progress and modification of all forms of human life and thought re-act on meanings. In the course of time such modifications of meaning amount to considerable sense-changes, even if the change is gradual and at any one moment hardly perceptible. (Stern 1931: 193)

2. Analogy, defined by Høffding as "identity of relations between separate objects, not identity of the single characteristics" (Stern 1931: 199), is primarily unintentional. Stern distinguished between combinative and correlative analogy, the former including flexional and derivational factors, e.g. OE *eolr* 'a man of noble birth, rank' changed to ModE *earl* 'the governor of the greatest divisions of England'.

3. Shortening, which is the omission of a word or a syllable from a compound word or an expression, leaving the remaining part still carrying the total meaning that formerly belonged to the whole expression, e.g. German *Universität* changed to *Uni*, English *advertisement* changed to *ad*.

4. Nomination is, according to Stern (1931: 168), a transfer "in which a name is intentionally transferred from one referent to another". The scholar gives examples of change from proper names, place names or Christian names used to denote an object, units of measurement, products, etc., e.g. *ohm, volt, Wellingtons, camembert, china, Bordeaux*, etc.

5. (Regular) Transfer is an unintentional transfer of a name to denote another referent due to a certain similarity of features between the two. For instance, every saddle has certain characteristics. In fact it is 'a seat made of leather that is put on a horse's back so that someone can ride it' (*LDCE* 1978). However, this term can be used to denote a thing that resembles a saddle in shape or function: a depression in a hill, a long elevation of land with sloping sides, a ridge connecting two hills, a seat, etc.

6. Permutation is "a modification of the subjective apprehension of the referent. […] we have a shift in the point of view concerning a detail of a total situation, a detail of a phrasal referent, the same word being retained to denote it" (Stern 1931: 352), e.g. MidE *bede* 'prayer' changed to ModE *bead* (*to tell one's beads* 'to count the beads of the rosary').

7. Adequation is an adaptation of the meaning to the actual features of the referents which the word starts to denote. What is different between this type of classification and substitution is the fact that the reason for this alteration lies in the subjective apprehension of the speaker, e.g. *horn* 'one of the pair of hard pointed parts that grow on the heads of cows, goats and other animals' changed to *horn* 'a musical instrument'

The father of the functional typology of semantic change is Ullmann (1957). Giving the skeletal scheme of this classification, Ullmann distinguishes semantic changes due to linguistic conservatism and innovation. The latter ones yield three categories of meaning change:

1. Transfers of names:

   a) through similarity between the senses, best illustrated by metaphors, e.g. *apple of the eye, look with the evil eye, grain of truth*, etc.
   b) through contiguity between the senses, called metonymy, e.g. *The whole school was evacuated after the telephone call informing them about a planted bomb.*

2. Transfers of senses:

   a) through similarity between the names, e.g. Eng. *Caesar* > Ger. *Kaiser;*
   b) through contiguity between the names on the basis of shortening or ellipsis, e.g. *capital* from *capital city, minister* from *Cabinet Minister, port* from *port wine;*
   c) composite transfers, which represent the borderline cases that can be equally attributed to more than one of the above categories, e.g. *Rembrant,* which can be both the author and the product.

It is noteworthy that as far as the axiological or evaluative classification is concerned, there is no single name in favour of this typology of sense alteration. The present trend was triggered in 1863 by Reinhold Bechstein with his work *Ein pessimistischer Zug in der Entwicklung der Wortbedeutung,* which soon aroused a great interest among other scholars, such as Müller (1865), Trench (1892), McKnight (1925), Schreuder (1929), Dongen (1933), etc.

It is clear that some words in their developments and acquisition of new evaluative meanings either start being semanticised with a negative connotation, or conversely are elevated. Therefore, two categories of axiological classification can be distinguished:

1. Amelioration – the tendency of a word to semanticise more positive connotations. This trend attracted McKnight's (1925) and Van Dongen's (1933) attention. Ameliorative developments, as a kind of specialisation, can be illustrated with OE *cniht* 'a boy, youth, lad', which changed to ModE *knight* 'a man with a high rank in former times who was trained to fight while riding a horse'.
2. Pejoration – the tendency of a word to employ more negative connotations. Such degeneration of meaning is one of the most common kinds of semantic change and considered much more emotive in nature than amelioration). The study of words falling into disrepute was dealt with by Schreuder (1929), e.g. OE *cnafa* 'a male child, boy', which changed to MidE *knave* 'a dishonest person, a rouge'.

1.5.2 Semantic change: causes and conditions

Having discussed the typologies of semantic change, it seems reasonable to specify their causes. As above, the matter does not resolve itself into one simple point of view. For this reason, let me start with two mutually complementary theories introduced in the 1920s.

One of them was put forward by Meillet (1921), who came with three ultimate causes of sense shifts:

1. linguistic reasons, where words are linked in a linguistics context, e.g. the French word *pas* 'step', originally positive in meaning, reinforced the French negative marker *ne*, and consequently acquired a negative meaning. Primarily, it was *ne pas* that carried negation in French, today *pas* alone, as a result of language economy, is a negation itself;
2. historical reasons, where a change results from a change in the object referred to, or a change of the speaker's perception of the object concerned e.g. the French word *plume* originally meant 'feather', then 'a writing instrument made from a feather', whereas now it is 'a writing instrument';
3. social stratification, i.e. the influence of languages or dialects on one another, e.g. Lat. *ponere* 'to put' brought French *ponder* 'lay eggs' into existence.

Sperber (1922), on the other hand, proposes a psycho-analytical approach to the issue. He introduces the notion of *fixative factor*, i.e. the one which is required if most of the individual decisions taken for generalisation of meaning follow the same direction. Thus, on the basis of semantic changes, Sperber introduces two major kinds of sense alterations:

1. non-affective changes due to ellipsis, name giving, modifications in the referent;
2. affective changes due to:
   a) the speaker's own feelings (expansion, attraction);
   b) the speaker's regard for the hearer's emotions (euphemisms).

Ullmann (1957) attributes semantic causes to pejorative tendencies, the importance of filling gaps in the lexicon, the evolution of referents, artistic delight, taboo influences, and semantic imitation.

Waldron (1986), in turn, presupposes similar factors of semantic change, i.e. changes in the world at large, emotional feelings, moral attitudes, "the constant traffic in words" (p.117), successive waves of borrowings.

The issue of causes of semantic change was also taken up by Kamboj (1986), who divides these causes into two groups, i.e. linguistic and extra-linguistic. The former is due to phonetic changes, the influence of foreign languages, reborrowing, remotivation, analogy or just the need for a new name. The latter are changes due to religious factors, social, cultural and economic shifts, as well as changes in geographic conditions.

The beginnings of diachronic semantic research neither stated any difference between the causes of semantic changes and their conditions, nor focused on these issues themselves. It was Stern (1931) who first distinguished between these causes and the conditions of semantic change and proposed an explicit description of their phenomena, taking into account various change typologies. The same view was later adopted by Ullmann (1957) who produced the following statement:

> The ultimate causes of semantic change must be kept apart from the conditions underlying them. The latter make semantic modifications possible, they provide ready-made patterns for them, without actually setting them off, or determining their form (Ullmann 1957:187).

1.5.3 Semantic change: laws and mechanisms

Since, from the viewpoint of diachronic semantics, language is considered to have a cohesive and regulating force, some effort was made to establish the rules and laws of semantic change. However, no consensus has been reached either on the ultimate definition of any principle of sense shift, or on the very existence of such principles.

Meillet (1921) claimed that it is impossible to establish any rules of semantic change, since every word develops in its own characteristic way. A similar viewpoint was represented by Weisgerber (1927) and Schuchardt (1928). However, other authors were convinced that semantic laws must exist. According to Ullmann (1957: 249), the understanding why meanings become extended or restricted comes from the comparative study of languages. Therefore, Schuchardt (1928), being convinced of the ambiguity of the notion of semantic change, proposed triple *petitio principii* as a solution to the problem:

1. all sound-laws are of a spatio-temporal variety (he mentions the necessity of the period, the area, and the set of conditions for the change);
2. all linguistic laws have to employ this rule;
3. no semantic developments are amendable (in Ullmann 1957: 252).

In a similar vein, on the basis of his analysis of the historical development of MidE adverbs in which *rapidly* changed its meaning into *immediately*, Stern (1931) postulated the following view:

> English adverbs which have acquired the sense 'rapidly' before 1300, always develop the sense 'immediately'. This happens when the adverb is used to qualify a verb, the action of which may be apprehended as either imperfective or perfective, and when the meaning of the adverb consequently is equivocal: 'rapidly/immediately'. Exceptions are due to the influence of special factors. But when the sense 'rapidly' is acquired later than 1300, no such development

takes place. There is no exception to this rule. This 'law' has the form of a sound-law: it gives the circumstances of the change and a chronological limit' (Stern 1931: 190).

To sum up, diachronic semantics is about describing, not explaining, changes in meaning. This is because, due to its structuralist nature, the diachronic approach presupposes that words are organised into semantic fields – it is to this issue that we turn in the next section.

1.5.4 Lexical relations in the context of diachronic semantic change

As has been shown in the previous sections, lexical items in a lexical field are inevitably connected with one another due to a variety of relations, either semantic or formal ones. The question we want to ask now is that of the correlation of those relations with the evolution of lexical fields.

First of all, along the lines of Guiraud (1976: 13), meaning is a process that associates an object/event with a sign that can evoke it. Therefore, we can suspect that the meaning *a* of the lexical item *x*, due to a similarity, part-whole relation, etc. with another lexical item *y* whose meaning is *b*, not necessarily from the same lexical field, becomes inevitably mentally linked to sense *b* of the lexical item *y*. However, what needs to be mentioned in the context of the forthcoming discussion is the fact that once we start such mental associations, consciously or subconsciously, relations between lexical items are created, which can largely contribute to a change of the meaning of one of the items, or even its loss. After all,

> a sense undergoes changes because we consciously give concepts names for cognitive or evaluative purposes. We name things. A sense undergoes changes because one of our associations – as a secondary one – gradually shifts towards the elementary sense and takes its place. As a result, the sense evolves. (Guiraud 1976: 56; transl. Żyśko). [21]

Therefore, our mental associations connected with any object cause a particular meaning of a word, designating that object, to exhibit links to another lexical field. Bearing this in mind, one needs to remember that, as Durkin (2009: 224) notes, the study of sense change involves:

a) the study of the relations between different meanings of a word;
b) the study of the relations between different words and their senses;

---

21 [s]ens ulega zmianom, ponieważ świadomie nadajemy nazwy pojęciom w celach poznawczych lub ekspresywnych; nazywamy rzeczy. Sens ulega zmianom, ponieważ jedno ze skojarzeń – jako wtórne (…) – przesuwa się stopniowo w kierunku sensu podstawowego i wchodzi na jego miejsce; sens ewoluuje (Guiraud 1976: 56).

c) the analysis of the relations between the linguistic meaning and the cultural, social and psychological background of its usage.

Before we proceed to discuss semantic alterations within lexical fields in detail, as explored by scholars following the principles of historical semantics, let me deal with meaning changes, as exemplified by synonymous and antonymous relations.

On many occasions the history of language has proved that synonyms drift in opposite directions, either developing their own specialised meanings or resulting in the disappearance of one of the pair-words. Let us illustrate this with animal/cuisine terminology. Before the Norman Conquest, the Anglo-Saxon *cow, pig* and *deer* were terms denoting both the animals and their meat in the culinary context. The year of 1066 brought new words into English: *beef, pork* and *venison*, which were used in exactly the same sense. However, since "words must contrast with other words in order to be meaningful" (Murphy 2003: 205), the lexical items specialised their meanings. Therefore, the French terminology started to be used in the culinary context, whereas the Anglo-Saxon words were applied to the pastoral setting.

In the case of antonymy, Murphy (2003: 206) maintains that antonyms tend to be either culturally or psychologically motivated. For example, since the term *mail* has started to behave like a hyperonym to *e-mail* after the introduction of electronic mail, the term *e-mail* encouraged the appearance of the new coinage of *snail-mail*. Consequently, *e-mail* and *snail-mail* have become morphologically related antonyms. Another example Murphy (2003: 206) comes up with is the psychologically grounded word pair *homosexual : heterosexual*. As the linguist suggests, the latter term was coined in response to the former to highlight the difference in people's sexual orientation. What is more, while considering canonicity, i.e. the relationship that is measured in terms of a pair's co-occurrence in natural language as well as in set idiomatic expressions (e.g. *as different as night and day*), it carries an additional field when a metaphorical shift among the fields makes both words appropriate. How is this possible? Murphy's answer (2003: 208) is the following:

> [I]f we play the game where I tell you are *hot* or *cold* depending on how near you are to a hidden object, *hot* and *cold* make good opposites because the players imagine that the hidden object metaphorically radiates heat. Where the entire field is not part of the metaphor, other senses of the canonical opposite often interfere with its extension to the additional field.

However, let me now briefly deal with the notion of enantiodromia, as analysed by Murphy (2003: 209), which is the process replacing a word's meaning with the opposite meaning. Murphy gives the example of the term *bad*, which in American slang has been applied to mean 'good'.[22] Thus, the word remains in the same semantic field, but it refers to the other pole on the same scale when used literally.

To conclude, lexical relations between various meanings of a word, as well as the relations between the meanings of different words must be taken into consideration while exploring the notion of semantic change. Furthermore, these two kinds of relations seem to be influenced by extralinguistic factors, which, on many occasions, act as the driving force of semantic change. Therefore, if we accept Geeraert's (2010: 80) definition of the meaning of a word as "the total set of meaning relations in which it participates", then it is evident that the process of semantic alteration is a common and frequent one, stimulated by a change of mental associations, which, consequently, lead to a change of meaning relations. We thus now proceed to examine semantic changes in various lexical fields.

1.5.5 Diachronic semantic changes within semantic fields

As we understand Heraclitus' panta rhei 'everything flows', the only thing that is constant is change. This phrase has been expressed in different ways. For instance, according to Hussey (1947: 445), "nothing is static forever in nature; change is going on everywhere". So it is with language and word meanings. Hence, it comes as no surprise that many approaches to the study of sense shifts have been adopted. Actually, it would be true to state that whenever there is a discussion about a change of sense, the historical aspect of meaning is taken into consideration. Kleparski and Rusinek (2007a: 80) say that although "the issue of the historical evolution of lexical meaning has received various degrees of attention[,] (…) meaning alterations have always been a part and parcel of the history of any natural language".

It is Trier (1931) who started the relentless pursuit of semantic changes:

> [...] all the processes which alter the quantum of wordstock may be studied under two headings: 1) loss of vocabulary items and 2) rise of new words. It is definitely more difficult to discuss the question of loss than that of rise of new words since they usually 'die' slowly and it is hardly possible to delimit objectively and precisely the exact moment when they are gone. [...] We assume a general rule that words enter language in response

---

22 Spears (2000: 12–13) claims that *bad*, in the contemporary street usage, means 'suitable excellent', as in the following examples: *That is a bad man dancing there* or *Look at those really bad shoes on that guy*. Thorne (2007: 19), in turn, attempts to explain the background of such a semantic alteration. The change can apparently be attributed to the poorest black Americans who, probably ironically, employed the term *bad* in the sense 'good' to refer to anything that is bad for the white but good for the black. We owe the spread of the new meaning of *bad* to jazz, and later on to rap and hip hop music.

to a need; they disappear, either suddenly or gradually, when they are no longer needed
and/or there are new formations, more apt to fulfil the functions set to them. In other
words, their 'life' is a linguistic and extralinguistic measure of the necessity and/or pref-
erence of the needs of man. (Kleparski 1983: 4)

Hence, when it comes to the types of field modifications, Lyons (1977: 255) claims
that while comparing two historically distinct lexical fields covering the same conceptual areas, one might come up with a cluster of five different combinations:

1) there is no change either in the lexemes included in the field, or in the relations that hold among them:

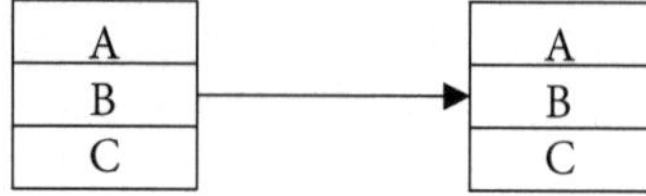

2) one of the lexemes is replaced with another one, maintaining the internal
   structure of the field:

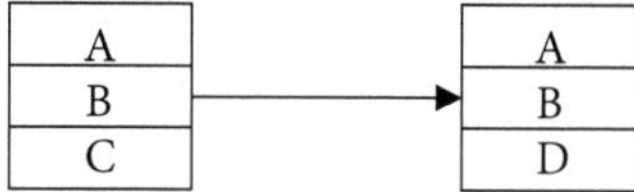

3) there is an alteration in the internal structure of the field, leaving the set of
   lexemes unchanged:

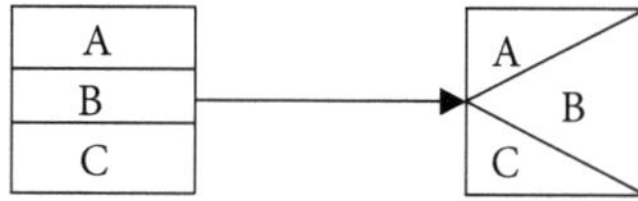

4) there is both a change in the internal structure of the field and a replacement
   of one of the lexemes:

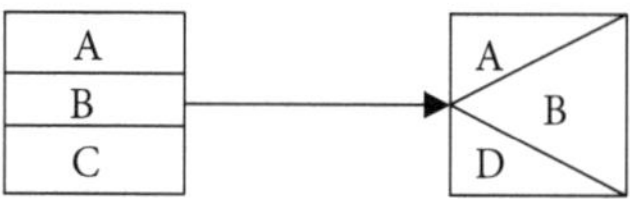

5) at least one of the lexemes has been added or lost with a change of the internal
   structure of the field:

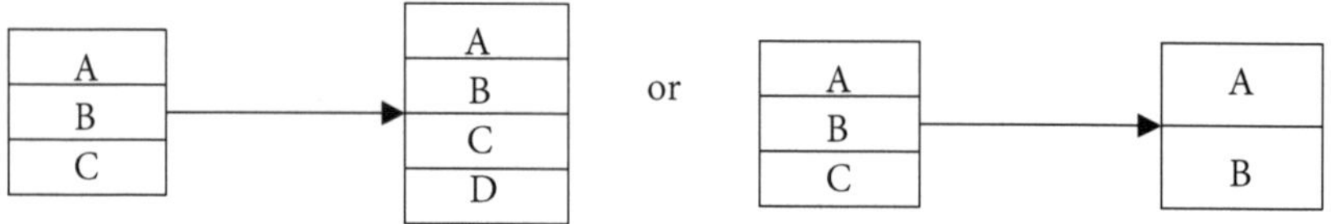

As Guiraud (1976: 56) maintains, first, the change is individual and conscious. A meaning changes on the basis of our mental associations because we deliberately, consciously give names to objects, notions, or people. Then, during the second stage, the change becomes collective, unconscious and continuous. This is because our secondary association moves toward the primary meaning and, consequently, changes it. As a result the sense evolves. This cognitive attitude towards the motivation mechanisms behind semantic changes leads us to believe that

> [t]he trick of being innovative and at the same time understandable is to use words in a novel way the meaning of which is self-evident" and "there are only two ways of going about that: using words for the near neighbours of the things you mean (metonymy) or using words for the look-alikes (resemblars) of what you mean (metaphor)." (Nerlich and Clarke 1992: 137)

1.6 Conclusion

To sum up, this chapter showed the correlation between semantic fields, understood as a structural way of grouping vocabulary together, and diachrony, i.e. language change. Consequently, the notion of a semantic field has been described, as well as the development of field theory. Quoting Murphy (2003: 95–96):

> field theory is a theory (or family of theories) of lexical (rather than conceptual) organization, which can be used to make weak claims about associative meaning (relations partly determine meaning), but it is often used to discover or illustrate componential analyses of lexical meaning. (…) While field theory has 'proved its worth as a general guide for research in descriptive semantics' (Lyons 1977: 267), its value is precisely in describing and not in explaining.

Accordingly, notwithstanding the fact that field theory is perceived as a description rather than explanation of the way vocabulary items are organised within a semantic field, we cannot reject its postulates. Although structuralist in nature, they surely form the underpinnings of contemporary cognitive linguistics and its explanation of vocabulary grouping and change.

Apart from field theory, Chapter 1 discussed the peculiarities of diachronic semantics, which is the study of language change that describes the change rather than explains the processes that govern semantic developments. Structurally-oriented diachrony does not involve motivation to account for words being related in semantic fields, which cannot be accepted by the modern functionally-oriented cognitive approach to language, especially within the framework of panchrony as a study of language change. Therefore, the present book is not constructed around structurally-oriented semantic fields as a description of diachronic changes in word semantics, but around a functionally-oriented cognitive approach to language and a panchronic attitude to semantic change. In Chapter 2 we focus on precisely these issues: cognitive linguistics and panchrony.

Chapter 2: Cognitive Linguistics and Panchrony

2.1 Introduction

We have seen so far that one possible way of grouping lexical items can be captured in terms of semantic fields, or, as we try to redefine it in Chapter 2, cognitive domains. The question we want to ask now is that of the motivating forces behind suchlike groupings. In other words, if we have a group of words that we can bring together into a homogenous set, there must be some explanation for doing so, some well-justified and well-grounded reason why this is at all plausible. The justification for this line of research now comes from functionally-oriented linguists, such as Ronald Langacker (2008: 88; emphasis changed):

> It is not a matter of deciding categorically whether a certain combination is or is not grammatical, but rather of ascertaining the kind and degree of *motivation* it has in view of all relevant factors. Hence the dictum in cognitive linguistics is that, while virtually everything is *motivated*, very little is subject to absolute predictability.

Langacker (1987, 1988, 1990, 1991, 1994, 1998, 1999, 2002, 2008, 2009, 2011a, 2011b, 2015) seems to be saying that while relating words to each other within a certain set, there may be both different causes for the relevant relations and different degrees of these causes.

To give a preliminary example of what we are in search of, in Rusinek (2009: 90–91) I discuss the grouping of *basque* 'the continuation of a waistcoat, now only of a lady's bodice slightly below the waist, forming a kind of short skirt', *Bloomers* 'baggy trousers gathered at the ankle and worn with a short skirt', *cardinal* 'a short cloak worn by ladies, originally of scarlet cloth with a hood', *middy* 'a loose blouse with a sailor's collar worn by women', *reefer* 'a man's short close-fitting coat made of thick material' and *toreador* 'women's tight-fitting trousers, tapering to mid-calf' (after *OED* 1971). They all have to do with the domain of OUTER GARMENTS, which may be considered to be a sub-set of the domain of CLOTHES. However, when we ask the question why we bring these six items together, there may be different answers, each specifying a different reason.

First of all, let us note that the reason for putting them together has little to do, if anything at all, with the parameter of shape/form. If *Basque* is a skirt, *cardinal*, *middy* and *reefer* cover the top, and *toreador* is a kind of trousers. Moreover, even if we try to justify *bloomers* and *toreador* together, the design difference is that the former is baggy, but the latter is not. Positively, the binding factor is that of function.

More importantly, we put all the six under one and the same rubric for methodological reasons, which is the direction in which their semantic evolution has taken place over the centuries. To be precise, all these aforementioned lexical items have evolved from the domain HUMAN BEING to the domain CLOTHES. Such a direction of semantic evolution is due to the fact that certain categories of human beings were originally associated with people, but with time became associated with these wearers to such an extent that they were given the wearers' names.

Since associations and impressions are the matter of an individual's conceptualisation, the aim of the present chapter is to discuss cognitive linguistics and its major principles in order to highlight the role of cognitive domains, not structural semantic fields, in the grouping of words and their senses. In addition, dealing with the notion of semantic change, we now juxtapose structural diachrony with the functionally and cognitively oriented panchrony. As a result, we see that semantic developments are motivated by cognitive processes in the human mind, captured under the umbrella notion of conceptualisation. Thus, not only can changes in meaning be described, but, more importantly, they can be explained.

2.2 The major characteristics of cognitive linguistics

Cognitive linguists and cognitive scientists, working in related research traditions, have proposed a number of theoretical constructs for cognitive linguistic theories of semantics and grammar. While non-cognitivist linguistics views meaning as being reduced to the content of a linguistic expression considered objectively, cognitive linguistics equates meaning with conceptualisation, and hence takes into consideration the subjective impact on the part of the individual. Of course, the context of a linguistic expression is described linguistically and, moreover, it focuses on subjective influences such as expectations, assumptions, cultural origin, perception, etc. One immediate advantage of this theory is that lexical and grammatical systems are complementary to each other in meaning construction and comprehension. This makes grammar equally important to lexis while expressing meanings (for Langacker, grammar is symbolic in nature). The cognitive approach to language is aptly summarised by Fauconnier (1988):

> Language does not link up directly with a real or metaphysical world; in between takes place an extensive process of mental construction, which does not mirror either the expressions of language responsible for setting it up, or the real world target situations to which it may be intended to apply. (Fauconnier 1988: 62)

It is thus evident that it is the background of a person's beliefs, practices or experiences that makes it easier to comprehend the meanings of words, whereas understanding the background enables them to know the meaning.

I shall now turn to the discussion of the three approaches to cognitive linguistics distinguished by Ungerer and Schmid (1996: x-viv), which might prove helpful while characterising meanings of linguistic expressions, and serve as an introduction to further cognitive linguistic inquiries.

The first approach, the *experiential view*, draws considerably from the empirical aspect of human subjective experience rather than from logically strict and objective definitions, rules and orders. Obviously, it is of paramount importance for the view to incorporate the individual's personal impressions, associations and feelings more readily than those attributes that constitute the general, communal experience of the whole speech community. Moreover, it is the experience of the so called "average person" and the way they perceive the world that is of great interest for Ungerer and Schmid. Personal knowledge and life experience might prove helpful while characterising, recognising and/or identifying objects as similar to others that the individual has encountered – such is the basis of categorisation, one of the major human cognitive abilities. It should be emphasised that, as the cognitive linguists assert, the experience of the world that is shared by a society or community may influence everyday language use and, by these means, be stored in the society or community. However, one further point should be made in connection with this – it is cognition that plays the most significant role in structuring experience(s).

Of no less importance for Ungerer and Schmid (1996) is the corresponding *prominence view* of linguistic structures. Its basis is the degree of prominence of different elements, which arranges and selects the information in a given situation. In view of the above considerations, this may have profound implications on the description of the circumstances of the given activity or situation which, in fact, influences the feelings and emotions of both the speaker and the listener.

The third view is the *attentional view*. The attempt to characterise particular parts of a situation or event is based on that aspect of the event which attracts the greatest attention and interest of the individual, for the purpose of comprehending and expressing one's construal of the situation. Moreover, this view explains why certain parts of the event are not mentioned in an utterance: apparently they are not considered sufficiently worthy of attention.

2.3 Cognitive Grammar

One of the most prominent figures in cognitive linguistics is Ronald Langacker (1987, 1988, 1990, 1991, 1994, 1998, 1999, 2002, 2008, 2009, 2011a, 2011b, 2015), the author of a global cognitive model of language description called Cognitive

Grammar. The model opened a new era in linguistic studies due to its innovatory attitude towards grammar, its nature and relation to other dimensions of linguistic structure. Hence, grammar ceases to have "a bad reputation. (…) [It also stops to represent] the danger of being criticized for breaking arcane rules [people] can never quite keep straight" (Langacker 2008: 3). Therefore, grammar enters a new phase of its perception since Langacker does not treat it as "a system of arbitrary forms based on abstract principles unrelated to other aspects of cognition of human endeavor" (ibid.). For Langacker, grammar is inherently semantic and symbolic, just as is the lexicon. The meaningfulness of grammar is twofold. First of all, the elements of grammar have their own symbolic significances. Secondly, it is grammar that allows us to construct and symbolise meanings of more complex expressions. Thanks to being meaningful, it becomes

> an essential aspect of the conceptual apparatus through which we apprehend and engage the world. And instead of being a distinct and self-contained cognitive system, grammar is not only an integral part of cognition but also a key to understanding it. (Langacker 2008: 4)

Thus, we are right to state that grammar, just as words, involves conceptualisation, which, in turn, is grounded in physical reality and social interaction. Grammar, therefore, is based on the interlocutors' thoughts, knowledge and intentions. Furthermore, as it can be inferred from the above considerations, grammar, being viewed as psychologically plausible and empirically viable, reflects our experience. Thus, since meaning is embodied in conceptualisation, Cognitive Grammar is not only conceptual, but also embodied.

When it comes to the symbolic nature of language, as defined by Langacker (2008), let us quote Łozowski (2010):

> Ronald Langacker treats the symbolic character of grammar as the most fundamental of his assumptions, reducing all linguistic structures to the pairing between phonological and semantic structure in the form of symbolic structures. (Łozowski 2010: 91; transl. Żyśko)[23]

Łozowski also pays attention to the issue of the roots of Langacker's theory. As the former mentions, "answering the question of the roots of his theory, Langacker directly says that "it is neither a direct continuation nor a dimension of

---

23 Ronald Langacker istotnie za najbardziej fundamentalne ze swoich stwierdzeń podaje symboliczny charakter gramatyki, redukując tym samym wszelkie konstrukty językowe do połączeń struktur fonologicznych i semantycznych właśnie w postaci struktur symbolicznych.

any linguistic theory"""[24,25]. In an interview conducted by Maldonado (2004: 305), Langacker signals that the development of his Cognitive Grammar has greatly benefited from his own contact with the Uto-Aztecan family of Native American. In fact, "[t]he diachronic and cross-linguistic perspective this afforded has been very useful".

Let us also note that since language is grounded in social interaction, it has, from the viewpoint of Cognitive Grammar, a decidedly interactive character. Furthermore, for Langacker language is also localist. All in all, bearing in mind the fact that all these aforementioned issues can be considered as *functions* of language, this brings us to a discussion of functionalism as understood by cognitive linguists:

> [T]he functionality ascribed to language here is given in terms of the all-embracing postulate of non-autonomy (…), which, on our reading, embraces at least three general functionally-oriented claims: (i) of the prevalence of motivated symbols over arbitrary systems (…), (ii) of the primacy of expression (intent) over communication (context) (…), and (iii) of the precedence of function over structure (…)" (Łozowski 2008: 18).

The discussion of functionalism will be followed by that of the tenets of Langacker's Cognitive Grammar, as they are understood by the scholar himself and other researchers.

2.3.1 Cognitive Grammar as a functionalist approach to language

At the beginning of our discussion of the functionally-oriented approach to language, let us quote Evans and Green (2006: 759), who define it as

> any approach that places particular emphasis on the communicative and social functions of language, and attempts to explain the grammatical properties of language in terms of how it is used. In this respect, functional approaches tend to be less concerned with the psychological representation of language as a system of knowledge and more concerned with its use.

Since language is shaped by the functions it serves (Langacker 2008: 7), it is right to state that the functional approach to language is one of the key tenets of cognitive linguistics, standing in opposition to formalism (as an approach that concentrates on the formal side of language). To be precise, while the functional

---

24 Langacker (2002: 1).

25 „w odpowiedzi na pytanie o korzenie swojej teorii R. Langacker mówi wprost, że „nie jest bezpośrednią kontynuacją ani odmianą żadnej innej teorii językoznawczej‟‟ (Łozowski 2010: 91).

approach tends to treat functional considerations as foundational, the formal one perceives them as a secondary aspect.

But the notion of functionalism can be considered from a range of perspectives. First of all, it needs to be emphasised that the functions language serves consist of semiological functions, where conceptualisations are symbolised by means of sounds and gestures, as well as multifaceted interactive functions that involve expressiveness, communication, social communion and manipulation. Therefore,

> [w]ithin functionalism, cognitive linguistics stands out by emphasizing the semiological function of language. It fully acknowledges the grounding of language in social interaction, but insists that even its interactive function is critically dependent on conceptualization. (Langacker 2008: 7–8)

Hence, "language is viewed as an integral facet of cognition" (ibid.). Since Langacker (ibid.: 8–9) maintains that the functional approach is a framework for linguistic description, he distinguishes between a three-level pyramid while dealing with the components of a comprehensive functional theory:

1) the first and lowest level lists the resources that are indispensable for describing linguistic structures;
2) the second level "wraps" the space of possibilities of defining linguistic structures, so that they are collected in certain areas only. This is how the functional theory determines their degree of prototypicality;
3) the third and top level of the pyramid deals with

> functional explanations for empirical findings at the second level. Proposing such explanations (e.g. offering discourse motivation for aspects of clause structure) has been a basic occupation of functional investigation" (ibid., p. 9).

However, what needs to be remembered is the fact that "[i]t is only by combining the functional and the descriptive dimensions that we arrive at a full understanding of grammatical phenomena" (ibid.)

The explanatory value of the functional approach to language is also considered by Evans and Green (2006: 759–760), who, dealing with the functional-typological approach to grammar, state that functional typologists call on functional and cognitive explanations of linguistic universals of economy and iconicity. While it is economical for a language to tend to shorten the most frequently used forms, "[i]conicity refers to the way that language 'mirrors' experience" (ibid.). The characteristics of a functional-typological approach to grammar are summarised in Table 2.

Table 2. Characteristics of a functional-typological approach to grammar.

Characteristics of a functional--typological approach to grammar		
Assumptions	Objectives	Methodology
• Semantic map model • Cognitive economy • Iconicity • Variation in language is natural • Language is dynamic • Use shapes language • The properties of language can be explained on the basis of human cognition and language use	• To describe linguistic universals • To state generalizations in terms of implicational universals	• Large-scale cross-linguistic samples • Close attention to linguistic form

A very similar view of functionalism, though not grammatically-oriented, is presented by Saeed (1997: 299–300), according to whom functionalism implies both internal and external language principles. Hence, language relies on whatever goes in the human mind/body, which is whatever makes it exposed to experience. Thus, language is shaped not only by principles operating at its levels, like syntax, morphology, etc., but it is also influenced by different aspects of human life. In fact, this viewpoint is shared by Brinton and Traugott (2005: 9), who maintain that, from the functional perspective, language is "a set of general cognitive tendencies strongly shaped by language external influences". What is more, they suggest that the speaker's intention stands for the parameters that decide the structure to be used. Hence, as we can conclude, the form of the language structure is determined by its function, cf. Bright (1992: 38): "functionalist research is aimed at clarifying the relationship between form and function and at determining the nature of the functions which appear to influence grammatical structure".

Therefore, since communication between human beings is possible due to linguistic forms determined by their functions, the communicative function of language appears to be the driving force behind its use. Consider Butler and Taverniers (2008: 690):

> [The] central aim of functionalism is that language should be seen first and foremost as a system for communication between human beings and that the shapes which languages take are strongly conditioned by both the nature of human cognitive capacities and the sociocultural contexts in which language is used.

All things considered, the functionalist tradition is very much aligned with the cognitive approach to language in its appeal to extra-linguistic factors of cognition to explain language properties, as well as its focus on language function and form. Functional linguistics and cognitive linguistics have much in common; to be more precise, cognitive linguistics is best treated as a specific undertaking within the functionalist tradition (Langacker 2008: 7).

2.3.2 Meaning as conceptualisation

A major characteristic of the cognitivist approach to language is that language is conceptual in nature and that meaning equals conceptualisation (Langacker 2008: 4). In fact, this view can be treated as the cornerstone of the whole enterprise, one from which all the other, more specific, principles derive.

Dirven and Verspoor (2004: 13) point out that language dwells in the mind of its speaker. Consequently, a concept is "a person's idea of what something in the world is like". Conceptualisation, in turn, has its grounds in physical activity. This includes the activity of the brain, functioning as an integral part of the body, the latter being an integral element of the world. Hence, meaning resides in the mind, but minds differ from person to person: linguistic meaning is grounded in people's knowledge, thoughts, intentions, the interlocutors' social interaction, as well as a variety of other factors, like the speaker's age, sex, social status, culture, etc. Therefore, in the processes of comprehending language, as well as in its development, there are continual tensions between the individual and the communal factors. Language does reside in individual minds, but minds do not use language in isolation: on the contrary, they constantly engage in socially-grounded interactions.

What needs to be emphasised is the fact that Langacker (2008: 30) assumes that it is conceptualisation, not concept, that is associated with meaning:

> Conceptualization is broadly defined to encompass any facet of mental experience. It is understood as subsuming (1) both novel and established conceptions; (2) not just "intellectual" notions, but sensory, motor, and emotive experience as well, (3) apprehension of the physical, linguistic, social, and cultural context; and (4) conceptions that develop and unfold through processing time (…). So even if "concepts" are taken as being static, conceptualization is not. Langacker (2008: 30)

Conceptualisation, or the cognitive processing that produces linguistic meaning, can eventually be reduced to the neurological activity of the brain – this issue, however, lies beyond the scope of the present study.[26] But conceptualisation is a

---

26 Cf. Peng, F.C.C. (1985); Brown, Colin M. and Peter Hagoort (1999); Friederici, Angela D. (2002); Phillips, Colin; Kuniyoshi L. Sakai (2005).

dynamic entity: meanings change due to a variety of factors (technological progress, cultural and historical environment, speaker's experience). It is therefore appropriate to talk about *conceptualisations*, rather than *concepts*, the former term suggesting a greater degree of dynamism.[27] Moreover, conceptualisation involves not only the subject matter of language use, but also the context, our assessment of the interlocutors' knowledge, as well as their intentions (Langacker 2008: 29).

2.3.3 The symbolic alternative

Linguistic signs are the ways in which language encodes and externalises our thoughts and ideas (Langacker 1990). Symbols, i.e. conventional pairings of linguistic form and meaning, are the predominant type of signs encountered in language. Since symbols can function as morphemes (for example *dis-* in *distaste*), whole words (for instance *cat, run, tomorrow*) or strings of words (for example *He couldn't write a pop jingle alone a whole musical*), it is true to say that symbols are pairing of forms and meanings. Forms can be of different types: they can be written (an orthographic representation), spoken (a sound) or signed (a gesture in a sign language). Meaning, in turn, is "the conventional ideational or semantic content associated with the symbol" (Evans and Green 2006; 6). Therefore, bearing in mind the fact that the pairing of form and meaning is inextricably incorporated into the notion of the symbol, a symbol is often referred to as an assembly or a form-meaning pairing, established by convention. What is more, one needs to remember that while thinking about an entity, for instance a cat, one will mentally imagine that entity, i.e. a particular cat. However, the image of the referent that we get in our mind is only to represent the idea of the referent, not a particular person/object/place etc. Hence, one has good grounds to maintain that the term 'meaning' does not equal the notion of concept, the latter one being a particular mental representation of a symbol. Apart from that, Evans and Green (2006: 7) believe that concepts derive from perceptual information having its source in the world, i.e. from percepts, the range of which falls into a single mental image. Meanings, in turn, "encoded by linguistic symbols, refer to our projected reality (…): a mental representation of

---

27 This view comes under the more comprehensive rubric of *conceptualism*, which is "any theory of semantics which defines the meaning of a word or other expression to be the concept associated with it in the mind of the speaker and hearer" (Lyons 1977: 112). This approach stands in contrast to those which associate word meaning with its use, such as that represented by Wittgenstein or Quine (1987: 130): "Language is a skill that each of us acquires from his fellows through mutual observation, emulation, and correction in jointly observable circumstances. When we learn the meaning of an expression we learn only what is observable in overt verbal behavior and its circumstances".

reality, as constructed by the human mind, mediated by our unique perceptual and conceptual systems" (ibid., emphasis changed).

A similar vision of language as a symbolic system is proposed by Langacker (2002: xv), who suggests that

> The word symbol refers to the basic claim that language is inherently symbolic. That is, all valid grammatical elements and constructs are held to be symbolic in the sense of having both conceptual and phonological import.

According to the author, the symbolic relation is the one that links the phonological and semantic structures. In other words, whenever a particular expression is pronounced by an individual speaker, it reflects the fact that a phonological structure is given its meaning. As for phonological structure, it "refers to the overt manifestation of language, i.e. a linguistic expression in its material, or perceptible aspects" (Taylor 2002: 20). Despite the fact that the linguist is aware that language can be realised in different ways, i.e. also by written and signed forms, and "'phonological structure' needs to be understood sufficiently broadly so as to be able to accommodate these possibilities" (ibid.), he definitely restricts the sense of the term 'phonological structure' to denote sound structure only.

When it comes to semantic structure, it is understood as the meaning of an expression in a situational context since it also comprises pragmatic aspects of meaning. As far as symbolic relations are concerned, these hold between phonological and semantic structures, the best illustration of which is presented in Fig. 13, after Taylor (2002: 21).

Fig. 13. The three elements of a linguistic expression (after Taylor 2002: 21).

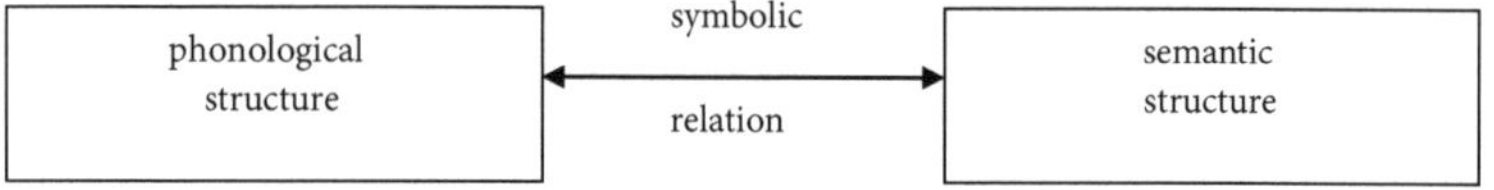

As can be seen in Fig. 13, the arrow points in both directions, which suggests that the relation between sound and meaning is a two-way issue. As Taylor (2002: 25) asserts, the conventionalised relation between phonological structure and semantic structure is given the name of a symbolic unit, which, as it turns out, exists not only on the level of a single lexical item, but also on the level of complex structures:

> [P]atterns for word combination (traditionally dealt with under syntax), as well as patterns for word formation (the province of morphology), are regarded as symbolic unit, each of which associates a phonological structure and a semantic structure. (Taylor 2002: 22).

There are three types of relations between symbolic units. These are:

a) the vertical relation that holds between units which differ in terms of a degree of detail. A unit which is more detailed is viewed as an instance of another unit, which, being less detailed, is schematic for the former;
b) the horizontal relation holds between sub-units of any unit that exhibits internal complexity;
c) the similarity relation causes units, though different, to become associated. Thus, if unit B is perceived to be similar to unit A, unit A is extended to unit B.

Furthermore, it should be noted that, since the semantic pole (S) and the phonological pole (P) can evoke each other, a symbolic structure (Σ) has a bipolar character, as can be seen in Fig. 14(a).

Fig. 14. Symbolic structures of language (after Langacker 2008).

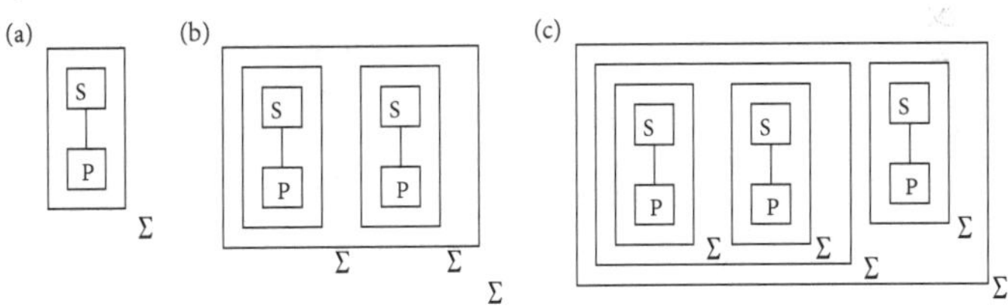

As is clear in Fig. 14(b), two symbolic structures can combine to produce a higher-level, complex symbolic structure, consequently constituting a symbolic assembly, sometimes elaborated to a high degree, as in Fig. 14(c). In order to illustrate combinations of symbolic structures, Langacker (2008: 16) gives the examples of *moon, moonless* and *moonless night*, respectively:

(a) [[MOON] / [moon]]
(b) [[[MOON] / [moon]] – [[LESS] / [less]]]
(c) [[[[MOON] / [moon]] – [[LESS] / [less]]] – [[NIGHT] / [night]]]

While units are enclosed in square brackets, hyphens are used for combinatory relationships, and slashes indicate symbolic relationships.

2.3.4 Embodiment

In cognitive linguistics, language is said to be embodied. Evans and Green (2006: 44) point out that the roots of the notion go back to the 17th century, when the French philosopher René Descartes developed the principle of mind/body dualism. In contrast to formal semantics, claiming that the mind and body as two distinct entities can be studied without recourse to one another, cognitive linguistics rejects the view that language can be studied without dealing with human experience or the nature of the human body. This is because

> [w]e live in a real world. Since our view of this world is mentally constructed on the basis of experience, each of us apprehends it somewhat differently[.] (…) [W]e always apprehend it at the present moment, from our current location, through our own senses, and with our own mental faculties. (…) Ultimately, the world we construct is grounded in our experience as creatures with bodies who interact with their surroundings through physical processes involving sensory and motor activity. (Langacker 2008: 524)

Thus, it is thanks to our anatomy and physiology that we can receive, interpret and understand sensory stimuli from the surrounding world. As a result, our physical acquaintance with the world produces mental images concerning the things we see, hear, touch, feel, smell and taste. To organise our experiences, we build so-called image schemas, e.g. of CONTACT, CONTAINER and BALANCE, which are meaningful because they are rooted in, and linked to, human pre-conceptual experience, i.e. experience of the world directly structured by the human body. Of all the things we can mentally experience thanks to our bodies, some appear as more salient and become generalised and entrenched in the form of schemas: fundaments for the emergence of concepts. Hence, since "our 'world view' (…) appears to us through the lens of our embodiment" (Langacker 2008: 48), reality is not perceived objectively but in a human-like manner: this is what Lakoff and Johnson (1980: 161) call experientialism or experiential realism.

But the way our mind acts, the way conceptual structure is embodied, also depends on social and cultural factors: embodiment thus has to do with much more than a mere body-world interaction, it has to do with the way we interact with the world as *cultural communities*. It is in this sense that our conceptual structure is inherited from the nature of our embodiment.[28]

2.3.5 The interactionist view

Langacker (2008: 7–8) underscores the fact that language is interactive in nature: it is integrated with extralinguistic factors shaping people's perception and thinking, such as communication, expressiveness, social communion and

---

28 But of course, of fundamental importance is the nature of our biological structure along with the peculiarities of the physical environment with which we deal. This, to a large extent, dictates our experience. Different organisms tend to have distinct kinds of experiences owing to the character of their embodiment (this is known as variable embodiment, cf. Evans and Green 2006: 45).

manipulation, etc. Therefore, cognitive linguistics "fully acknowledges the grounding of language in social interaction that even its interactive function is critically dependent on conceptualization" (ibid., p. 8). We do not live in isolation but are surrounded by others who, deliberately or not, influence our understanding of lexical categories. Therefore, meanings, being "actively negotiated by interlocutors on the basis of the physical, linguistic, social, and cultural context" (ibid., p. 28), dynamically emerge in social interaction and discourse. Meaning, thus, is due to the way information between speakers is passed. It cannot be seen as stored in an individual human mind but undergoes alterations under the influence of a range of cultural, social, and linguistic conditions.

According to Evans and Green (2006: 10–11), language can fulfil the interactive function in a few ways. First of all, the messages we pass can have social functions since we use language to "change the way the world is [5], or to make things happen [6]", as in the examples below:

(5) *I now pronounce you man and wife.*
(6) *Shut the door on your way out.*

As Evans and Green suggest, the utterance in (5), spoken in a given context by an appropriately qualified person, has the effect of changing the social and legal relationship between two people. In turn, with regard to example (6), we are right to state that not only does language allow us to express our wishes and desires, but it also makes it possible to signal what kind of relationship occurs between the speaker and his/her listener (e.g. *Shut the door on your way out* or *Would you be so kind and shut the door on your way out?*).

Secondly, the interactive function of language lets us express our feelings about the world. Evans and Green (2006: 10) give two examples of the notion of expressivity:

(7) *the eminent linguist*
(8) *the blonde bombshell*

Although both can denote the same person, they focus on different features of the woman concerned.

Thirdly, language can inform us about affect, i.e. someone's emotional reaction. Let us take into account the following sentences

(9) *Shut up!*
(10) *I'm terribly sorry to interrupt you, but...,*

They show that "[t]he language we choose to use conveys information about our attitudes concerning others, ourselves and the situations in which we find ourselves" (Evans and Green 2006: 11).

Last but not least, we use language to create scenes or frames of experience that demand reference to background knowledge, e.g.

(11) *How do you do?*
(12) *Once upon a time...*

It is evident from the utterances above that (11) invokes a greeting frame whereas (12) signals the beginning of a fairy tale.

To summarise, not only does language encode meanings, but it is also able to show their social, expressive and emotional aspects. The interactive function of language enriches its semantics in a variety of ways.

2.3.6 The localist view

The question cognitive linguists need to address here is whether meanings are localised in the minds of individuals or are "distributed over a speech community, the immediate context of speech, as well as the physical and sociocultural world" (Langacker 2008: 29). In our search for the answer, we need to distinguish between the variety of circumstances that make an interaction meaningful and the mental experience of an individual speaker who engages in the interaction. Therefore, when it comes to the influence from the surroundings, i.e. the context of an utterance, age, cultural background, sex, education and a range of other extralinguistic factors, Langacker (2008: 29) gives the example of *Open wide*, which is only fully comprehensible in the context of doctor-patient interaction, while examining the patient's throat. Outside this context, the utterance is vague or totally obscure. Therefore, meaning is the way a speaker understands an expression. In other words, it

> incorporates a speaker's apprehension of the circumstances and exploits the meaning potential they carry, but cannot be identified with those circumstances. So defined, an expression's meaning resides in the conceptualizing activity of individual speakers. (Langacker 2008: 29)

But do individuals really "know" the meaning of an expression? After all, scientific terms are differently understood by professionals dealing with them every day, and by laymen whose knowledge on certain subjects is superficial. In this case, claiming that meaning resides in the mind of an individual speaker would be wrong; instead, we should rather say that meanings are scattered over the speech community. So where are we: is meaning localised in the minds of individual speakers or does it have a distributed nature?

Langacker assumes that an expression's meaning is its meaning for a single speaker, but he does not diminish the social aspect of semantics. This is due to the fact that "[a]n individual's notion of what an expression means develops through communicative interaction and includes an assessment of its degree of conventionality in the speech community" (2008: 30). People acquire language by interaction with others; thus, its proper interpretation and understanding depends, to a large extent, on social factors shaping the interlocutors' lives. Therefore, it is impossible to explain semantic changes, i.e. to deal with panchrony, without taking into account these social factors.

2.4 The methodology of cognitive linguistics: basic concepts

In this section we will consider the issues relating to the methodology of cognitive linguistics. First of all, it needs to be pointed out that cognitive semantics should be differentiated from cognitive approaches to grammar, both tendencies being bifurcations of cognitive linguistics. The former (cf. Evans and Green 2006: 170) deals with analysing conceptual structures and the process of conceptualisation, which implies that meaning is studied not for meaning's sake, but rather for the knowledge it can give us about the nature of the human conceptual system. In other words, language serves as a tool for dealing with conceptual organisation. I will now proceed to discuss the methodological tools of cognitive linguistics.

2.4.1 Categorisation

Every human being possesses the ability to categorise. We categorise the environment in terms of good vs. bad, harmful vs. non-harmful, edible vs. non-edible. As Taylor (2002: 9) realises, we can create and operate thousands of categories, and are also able to modify already existing ones to accommodate new experiences. The same processes are feasible at the level of language. Langacker distinguishes two types of categorisation: categorisation by prototype, and categorisation by schema:

> A prototype is a typical instance of a category, and other elements are assimilated to the category on the basis of their perceived resemblance to the prototype; there are degrees of membership based on degree's of similarity. A schema, by contrast, is an abstract characterization that is fully compatible with all the members of the category it defines (so membership is not a matter of degree); it is an integrated structure that embodied the commonality of its members, which are conceptions of greater specificity and detail that elaborate the schema in contrasting ways." (Langacker 1987: 371)

Thus, a schema is an abstract template which represents the commonality of the structures it categorises (Langacker 1987: 71), and emerges as a result of our interaction with the world. According to Langacker (2008: 17–18), categorisation by schema is

> the interpretation of experience with respect to previously existing structures. A category is a
> set of elements judged equivalent for some purpose (…). If structure A belongs to a category,
> it can be used to categorize another structure, B, which may then become a category member.
> Categorization is most straightforward when A is schematic for B, so that B elaborates or
> instantiates A. (…) However, it can also happen that B conflicts with A's specifications but is
> nonetheless assimilated to the category on the basis of an association or perceived similarity.
> A is then a prototype (at least locally), and B an extension from it. (emphasis changed)

The other type of categorisation, according to Langacker (1987), is prototype categorisation, which was introduced into the scope of semantics by Eleanor Rosch, a psychologist, in the 1970s. Her research was devoted to experiments on focal colours with the aim of finding whether they derive from pre-linguistic cognition or from language. As Ungerer and Schmid (1996: 6–10) point out, she has validated the fact that the categorisation of natural phenomena consists of three main stages, i.e. choosing the stimuli, identifying and classifying entities, etc., and supplying them with appropriate names. In addition, it is worth noting in connection with this that her primary concern was to argue that natural categories are created when they are based on their "best examples", i.e. prototypes of the categories, and that the classification of other objects thoroughly depends on their sufficient resemblance to the prototype.

Let me now consider the fundamental assumptions of the notion of the prototype. For Taylor (1989: 59), a prototype is "the central member, or […] the cluster of central members of a category". A prototype may be also defined as "a schematic representation of the conceptual core of a category" (ibid.). It is essential for an individual to have a mental representation of the prototype, as it is then easier to identify the prototype in different contexts. Moreover, it is required to remember the fact that the prototype has been equated with the most typical instance of a given category, or an abstract set of features typical for a given category. As I have already mentioned, the identification and classification of objects, entities, etc., to given categories is due to their similarity to the prototype, which implies that the more similar to the prototype such objects, entities, etc. are, the more central the place in the category they occupy.

However, the question that Rosch (1975: 198) asks is whether less salient entities can be categorised on the basis of the prototype. This is the reason why her most fundamental method of experiments is the Goodness-of-Exemplar ratings, which show whether certain members of a category are typical of it or represent its "bad" example. In this context, Cruse (2011: 57) mentions eight cases on the rating scale, declaring that examples of objects, entities, etc. within a category are the following: "very good", "good", "fairly good", "moderately good", "fairly poor", "bad", "very bad", or are "not examples" of the category at all. The examples, of course, are or are not described in terms of certain attributes that can be defined as typical aspects of given categories. The question about their status was dealt with even in ancient times when Aristotle, distinguishing between the essence of things and their accidence, claimed that features have to be sufficient and necessary. However, cognitive linguistics has departed form the notion of categorisation based on necessary and sufficient conditions, but recognizes the fuzzy nature of their boundaries, which we will explore below.

Typicality ratings largely depend on the culture of a given society. Moreover, it is interesting to note that familiarity may have a great impact on the selection of typicality ratings, which was shown by Wittgenstein (1958: 66f). This Austrian linguist, having described the examples of the category 'game', came to the conclusion that categories are connected by a network of overlapping resemblances, which he referred to as 'family resemblances'. This implies that the different members of a category do not share all the common features/characteristics that might form the basis for distinguishing them from these objects that are not members of the category. Wittgenstein's interpretation of family resemblance is based on the observations of a human family, in which its members resemble one another. However, not all features are possessed by all of them. In addition, some members of such a family may not share any features at all, which implies, as Taylor (1989: 40–46) concludes, that, on the basis of the process of categorisation, different members of one and the same category may occupy not only a central, but also a peripheral, position.

Moreover, it should be noted that Rosch shows that the impossible, classic question "To what extent does this particular object, entity, etc. belong to a category?" is quite reasonable. She comes up with the idea of a degree of membership as a really valid notion in psychology, and claims that the statement that a prototypical object belongs to a category takes less time than in the case of a peripheral one. Simultaneously, it is vitally important to accentuate another important aspect of Rosch's experiments, i.e. the so called prototype effects, which are correlations between prototypicality, measured by typicality ratings, and cognitive behaviour. It is interesting to note that what influences the degree of membership exerts influence on the overall frequency and order of mentioning. It appears that when one is supposed to list a number of members of a given category under pressure of time, one usually tends to mention the prototypical member first. In addition, there is a strong tendency to list it more frequently, which is a consequence of the Goodness-of-Exemplar ratings. It should be noted that, as far as the order of acquisition and vocabulary learning is concerned, it is fair to say that it also corresponds to the Goodness-of-Exemplar ratings, and it is prototypes that are acquired first. Moreover, children tend to learn vocabulary consisting of prototypical instantiations faster than marginal ones.

It is noteworthy that the degree of membership also has an impact on priming. If a word is preceded by another word which is semantically related to it, and usually of a subordinate category name, the category name speeds up the occurrence of the prototype category (Cruse 2011: 59).

In Ungerer and Schmid's interpretation (1996: 14), Rosch argues that categories do not have boundaries but that the boundaries "at some unspecified point or area beyond their periphery (…) somehow fade into nowhere". However, as the two scholars state, one usually wants to draw a demarcation line between various categories. They also claim that it is essential to distinguish between vagueness and fuzziness. While the former often takes place when concrete entities, objects, etc. lack clear-cut boundaries in reality, the latter is applied to the borders between the categories of these entities that are fuzzy. This fact, in turn, does not presuppose that these two kinds of boundaries do not coincide with each other. From the viewpoint of cognitive linguistics, the discussion of vagueness is much less significant than that of fuzziness. It is obvious that it is only the prototype that possesses the whole one hundred per cent membership of a category, while the degree of membership of the other constituents depends on their Goodness-of-Exemplar ratings. From this, it follows that there are no fixed boundaries between categories: "There is no fixed limit on how far something can depart from the prototype and still be assimilated to the class if the categoriser is perceptive or clever enough to find some point of resemblance of typical instances" Langacker (1991: 266). This was shown by Labov (1973: 353), who, researching the category of cup and cup-like containers, showed that the fuzziness of category boundaries may be influenced by a given context.

Another important point should be made in connection with this. Ungerer and Schmid (1996: 60–66) highlight the fact that, as far as classification is concerned, especially classification of scientific objects, it is obvious that cognitive categories are interconnected with each other on the basis of their hierarchical organisation. This idea might be viewed from the point of view of class inclusion, which implies that categories possess the features that are characteristic of the dominating superordinate category, with an addition of features that are unique, typical of these superordinate categories, and which distinguish them from the other members of the subordinate categories. This is a matter of taxonomies (let us recall scientific taxonomies, introduced by Linnaeus). The factor of primary importance in scientific classifications is the objectiveness with which one should approach the entities being classified.

The fact that the classical model of categorisation represents a great deal of shortcomings has had significant consequences. First, categories do not always possess all the features that are typical of the superordinate categories and, what is more, certain features are peculiar to individual members of the category. Secondly, the levels of categorisation have not proved to be of equal status, and this implies that some of them have to be more salient than others. A level of categorisation which possesses this characteristic and the greatest number of correlated attributes is called the "basic level" of categorisation. In other words, it is a level which has a special status of specifity (Taylor 1989: 48). The basic level is also sometimes called the generic level. However, the former has a more psychological character. It appears that generic-level categories are especially connected with cultural and linguistic importance:

> [G]eneric-level categories represent the preferred cognitive perspective [and] seem to meet 'basic' cognitive needs because they pinpoint where the focus of human interest lies. Regarding their position within hierarchies, generic categories are characterised by 'taxonomic centrality'. (Ungerer and Schmid 1996: 66)

The terms from generic categories come to a person's mind not only more often than the peripheral members, but also first. One of the reasons for such a state of affairs is the fact that the names of basic level categories are usually morphologically simple and do not involve figurative language, whereas the names of more specific categories are rather complex. This, in turn, may even lead to a situation where they become obsolete. The basic-level items tend to be more frequently used in everyday situations in neutral matters, for they are considered by speakers to be the most appropriate and real names for a given object, entity, etc. Thanks to the fact that the attributes of basic-level categories are stored in one's mind, the basic level is easily accessed in the cognitive sense: this is the principle of cognitive economy.

Another point worth mentioning which has an influence on the primacy of the basic level is the fact that the level includes characteristic features of behavioural interaction, and is responsible for the formation of a clear visual image. It is obvious that an overall shape, which can be perceived holistically, comes down to representing gestalt principles. The basic level includes representatives which maximise internal homogeneity by underscoring the attributes that are common to all the members of a given category. Secondly, they maximise the distinctness from the categories they border, which is possible thanks to the fact that they minimise the number of attributes that are shared with the other categories. Thirdly, they also maximise differential informativeness. However, all these features are understandable in terms of encyclopaedic knowledge, which gives a person a unique insight into the characteristics of a category (Taylor 1989; Cruse 2011: 62).

Of unquestionable importance for an adequate description of the character of categories and the notion of categorisation is the problem of category types and their characteristics. Regarding the first one, I would like to determine the nature of superordinate categories. Taking into consideration the fact that the members of a given category do not all have the same shape, which means that, in terms of the gestalt, they are different and can be approached holistically. This is called parasitic categorisation: it involves the gestalt properties of the superordinate category taken from the basic-level categories, together with their names. In addition, as has been already mentioned, certain features are more salient than others. It is noteworthy that the most salient qualities of category members are their purpose and function (Labov 1973); therefore, highlighting such salient attributes is only to be expected of superordinate categories. Another effect is the collecting function of superordinate categories, which implies the gathering of plenty of categories under one label for better perceptive effects. Moreover, the third characteristic of superordinate category is its experiential hierarchy that has originated from folk taxonomies. From this, it follows that there might be some alternative ways, inconsistencies and gaps, because the cognitive capacities and abilities of individual people may vary.

2.4.2 Cognitive domains

The notion of the domain is an important construct in Langacker's Cognitive Grammar. While describing domains, the author concentrates on cognitive features, such as human experience and an individual's understanding of the world, postulating that domains are "necessarily cognitive entities: mental experiences, representational spaces, concepts, or conceptual complexes" (Langacker 1987: 147). That is why Langacker states that every experience is potentially a domain when its concept is mentioned. This may imply that a domain is "a context for the characterisation of a semantic unit" (ibid.) or, in other words, "any kind of conception or realm of experience" that helps "[t]o have a uniform way of referring to content" (Langacker 2008: 44). This is due to the fact that linguistic meaning consists of conceptual content and the construal imposed on the content.

Naturally, the discussion about the notion of domain and conceptualisation must include the semantic relationship between domain and concept. Clausner and Croft point out that the concept-domain relation takes place on the level of the relationship between the "knowledge in which a category exists (domain) and category members (concepts)" (Clausner and Croft 1999: 6), not between general categories. The result of such a concept-domain relation is the fact that any concept can function as the domain for another concept. Such a relationship, which is the embedding of domains as concepts in other domains, can be scaled down, according to Langacker (2008: 44–45), to the notion of basic and nonbasic domains. Basic domains cannot be reduced to more elementary notions. The most common examples are space, or various types of sense experience, such as "color space (the range of colors we are capable of experiencing), pitch (the range of pitches we can perceive), temperature, taste and smell, and so on" (ibid., p.44).

As he notes, basic domains are not concepts or conceptualisations; instead, they are "realms of experiential potential, within which conceptualization can occur and specific concepts can emerge" (ibid., 44–45).

When it comes to the notion of nonbasic domains, we again face here the problem of grouping vocabulary items. The most common instances of such a way of bringing words together is, as Langacker (2008: 45) mentions, sensory, emotive and motor/kinaesthetic experience, as well as the abstract products of intellectual operations. As Langacker notes, these range from minimal concepts (for example, RED), to more elaborate ones (for instance, the construction of the human body), to entire systems of knowledge (a good instantiation is everything we know about football). Langacker (2008: 45) gives the example of the concept APPLE, which incorporates the concept RED. The concept NECK, in turn, invokes the shape of the body, whereas BATTING AVERAGE is associated with both arithmetic and baseball. In the eyes of the linguist,

> [i]n cases of this sort, where one conception – asymmetrically – presupposes another as part of its own characterization, they are said to occupy higher and lower levels of conceptual organisation. (Langacker 2008: 45, emphasis changed).

Furthermore, it is important to note that one linguistic form, for instance a lexical item, may be described by more than one domain at the same time. The effect of such a characterisation is a domain matrix. In other words, a matrix is a set of domains presupposed by a concept. The domains, which are included in a domain matrix, may be more or less separable in experience. According to Langacker, domains are devices thanks to which the description and understanding of the world is plausible. This means that domains, from the viewpoint of Langacker, cover the totality of experience. What also should be mentioned in the context of these considerations is the fact that the conceptual matrix usually has a complex nature. Furthermore, domains of a complex matrix overlap one another, which is illustrated in Fig. 15, adapted from Langacker (2008: 48):

Fig. 15. A matrix of domains (adapted from Langacker 2008: 48).

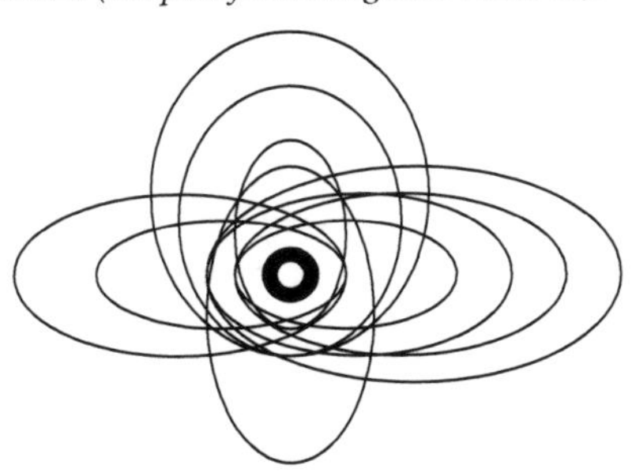

Langacker also refers to Fauconnier's (1997: 11) notion of mental spaces as "partial structures that proliferate when we think and talk, allowing a fine-grained portioning of our discourse and knowledge structures" (Langacker 2008: 50). Bearing in mind the fact that every day an average person tends to have a variety of associations, comparing different people, objects or ideas, to others previously acquired from experience, the number of newly produced metaphors can be huge. This is how Kardela (2007: 298) explains the process of conceptual blending:

> Two or more input spaces are connected with each other via so-called cross-space mapping. As a result, the third so-called generic mental space is created; this space contains all the elements that are shared by the input spaces. Finally, there is a fourth space, called the blend. The blend – and this must be stressed – is an emergent structure, created via the process of completion, whose elements are in neither of the inputs.

The blend-formation process is presented by him in the following way:

Fig. 16. Conceptual blending (adapted from Fauconnier and Turner 2002: 46).

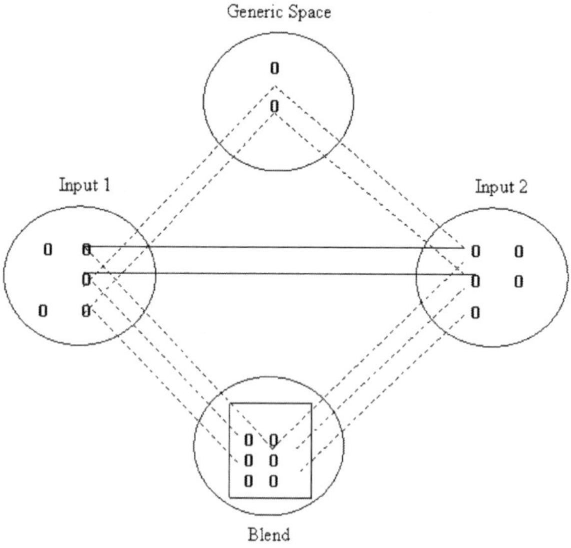

Generic Space

Input 1

Input 2

Blend

One notion important in the context of cognitive domain is that of entrenchment. This issue, introduced by Langacker (1987: 59), was originally used to explain how new expressions are formed and become rooted in the memory of their users (i.e. entrenched in the language they speak). Taylor (1989: 78) suggests that "membership in the category is released from otherwise highly entrenched, one might even say essential, attributes".

Linguists differentiate between core and complex entrenchments; the former equalling ORGANISING CONCEPTUAL CORE (OCC), the latter VARIANT CONCEPTUAL SPHERE (VCS). Furthermore, one of the domains associated with a given lexical item may be more salient than the others. That is why Langacker (1987: 165) points out that there are primary and secondary domains, the difference between which lies in the degree of typicality of a feature in the case of the lexical item. For instance, *Scarlett O'Hara* in its everyday sense is primarily associated with the domain of film heroines: she is a character from a legendary American cinematic masterpiece *Gone with the Wind*. Only secondarily is it an alcoholic mix of peach liqueur, cranberry and lime juice.

As has already been mentioned, the issue of grouping lexical items is an essential point to consider linguistically. The truth is that for centuries people associated certain portions of vocabulary together, claiming that there are certain connections between them. Therefore, thinking about the lexical item *apple,* one is tempted to mentally correlate it with, for instance, lexical items such as *pear, plum* or, extending the grouping of 'fruit' vocabulary to 'tropical fruit', with such items as *lemon, orange, banana,* etc. However, everyone's experience is somewhat different: while one person may associate this kind of fruit with the terms *baking, cake,* another individual may come up with quite distant concepts such as *love* or *childhood.* In fact, mental associations are unpredictable, yet dependent on one's experience. Thus, as is evident, the category *apple* goes beyond the borders of the structural semantic field FRUIT. Another instance of grouping words together is given by Rusinek (2008a, 2008b, 2009), who concentrates on 'clothes' terminology.

Let us recall that the structural linguistic tool for bringing words together is referred to as a semantic field. However, owing to linguistic research that judges cognition as the key to human thought, semantic fields proved to be a failure.[29] Therefore, looking at the issue concerned from the cognitive perspective, one has good grounds to state that the tool that mentally groups lexical items is a cognitive domain.

---

29 It is worth noting that the notion of the semantic field also fails as a factor of grouping words also in the eyes of Croft (1993: 337–338). He states: "It [the notion of domain] is related to the notion of a semantic field, as in the field theories of Trier and others. This work has come under considerable criticism, not least because the notion of semantic field is left undefined". The same viewpoint is shared by Lyons (1977: 267), who comments on the failure of field theory thus: "What is lacking so far, as most field-theorists would probably admit, is a more explicit formulation of the criteria which define a lexical field than has yet been provided".

2.4.3 Motivated organisation of domains

Bearing in mind Langacker's (2008: 44) belief in a strong semantic relationship between concept and domain, the latter defined as any kind of conception of experience, an individual's role in grouping words together becomes even more visible. This leads one to the question about the motivation for the organisation of domains. In one's search for an answer, one needs to take into consideration the notion of *sign*, which, according to Pierce (1992, 1998), is a method of expressing thought, and has three types: icons, indexes and symbols. These, it appears, differ in terms of a hierarchy of abstraction. The relationship between form and meaning in the three types of signs is presented in Fig. 17:

Fig. 17. The relationship between form and meaning in the three types of signs (adapted from Dirven and Verspoor (2004: 1–3).

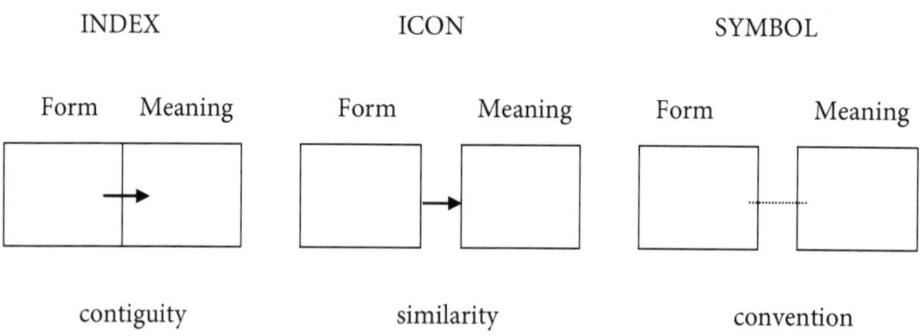

Importantly, the principles of indexicality, iconicity and symbolicity are cognitive ones. This is due to the fact that seeing the contiguity, resemblance or recognising the convention depends on the part of the interpreter/observer. Let me now discuss these principles.

An indexical sign, or index, reflects things that are contiguous. In other words, in the eyes of Taylor (2002: 45), "[a] sign is indexical if there is a natural connection between the signified and the signifier". This sort of sign, the name of which comes from Latin *index* 'pointing finger', points to something close. Since indexes are restricted to the 'here' and 'now', they are at the bottom of the abstraction hierarchy. As far as examples of this sort of sign are concerned, Dirven and Verspoor (2004: 2) suggest facial expressions such as raising one's eyebrows, which "points" to a person's internal emotional states of surprise.

An index, also referred to as a symptom, is a sign which stands for a relation between form and meaning which is either causal or presumed to be causal. It is believed that indexical signs are usually generated by natural events. To be specific, as Taylor (2002: 48) puts it, smoke is an index of fire, medical disorders are an index of a disease, raised pitch can be an index of agitation, etc. On the level of language, the principle of indexicality assumes that the entity at the centre of attention is the speaker himself/herself. Such an egocentric view of the world is revealed when we speak. Our position in space and time (*hic et nunc*) is considered to be the point of reference for the location of other entities in space and time. In the words of Dirven and Verspoor (2004: 5),

> [w]ords such as *here, there, now, then, today, tomorrow, this, that, come* and *go* as well as the personal pronouns *I, you* and *we* are described as deitic expressions. Deitic expressions relate to the speaking of EGO, who imposes his perspective on the world.

The term *icon* comes from the Greek *eikon* 'replica'. Hence, an iconic sign "provides a visual, auditory or any other perceptual image of the thing it stands for" (ibid.). For instance, the idea of danger caused by animals on roads is illustrated by icons, i.e. pictures of cows, horses, deer, etc. An iconic sign is also a picture of a holy person in the Orthodox Church. Due to the fact that iconic signs require the recognition of similarity, they are perceived as more complex in the hierarchy of abstraction. After all, the resemblance needs to be consciously established by the observer.

Dealing with the principle of iconicity, it is important to distinguish between imitative iconicity, structural iconicity, sequential iconicity and iconicity of proximity (Taylor, 2002: 46–47). Imitative iconicity plays a marginal role in linguistics. The reason for such a state of affairs is the fact that this sort of resemblance holds between words whose pronunciation suggests their meanings, i.e. the rather infrequent onomatopoeic words (*hiss, splash, cuckoo*). As for structural iconicity, what is taken into consideration is the correspondence of the structure of a phonological form to its semantic structure. For instance, plural nouns are usually longer than their corresponding singulars. The length of an utterance or sentence can also be considered: a longer sentence tends to give more details concerning the concept. Dealing with sequential iconicity, called the principle of sequential order by Dirven and Verspoor (2004: 8), it should be noted that it

> manifests itself in the order in which clauses are spoken. Generally, when narrating a series of events, a speaker will strive to mention the events in the same order in which they occurred. *They married and had a child* would be interpreted as narrating two events which took place in that order (Taylor, 2002: 47)

Iconicity of proximity, in turn, deals with things that are related conceptually and tend to be phonologically similar. According to this principle, the object appears adjacent to the verb, immediately before or immediately after. An intervening adverbial is not allowed, as in the following sentence: *The book is under the double – I think – bed.*

When it comes to a symbolic sign, or symbol, it stands on the top of the abstraction hierarchy. This can be explained by the fact that it goes beyond the limitations of contiguity and similarity. In other words, "[a] sign is symbolic if the reflection between the signified and signifier is established by convention" (Taylor, 2002: 45). This makes it possible to view a rose as a symbol of love.

2.4.4 Construal

Every symbolic structure construes its content in a certain way: viewing a scene depends on a number of experiential factors. Thus, it depends on what we examine, how closely we examine it, which elements attract our greatest attention, as well as the place from which we view it. In other words, as Langacker (1988: 7) states, we have an "ability to mentally 'construe' a situation in alternative ways. (…) In choosing a particular expression or construction, the speaker construes the conceived situation in a certain way". Therefore, taking into account our abilities to construe or imagine a situation, the process of structuring a particular state of affairs by a language, for purposes of its linguistic expression, has been given the name of construal or imagery (ibid.). Langacker (2008: 55) claims that construing the conceptual content of an expression's meaning is, to a great extent, associated with such dimensions as specificity, focusing, prominence and perspective. Since these constitute the fundamental methodological apparatus of cognitive linguistics, let us now discuss it from a closer perspective.

2.4.4.1 Specificity and schematicity

Specificity, sometimes referred to as granularity or resolution, is a dimension of construal that defines "the level of precision and detail at which a situation is characterized" (Langacker 2008: 55), For instance, *aunt* is more specific than *relative*. In other words, as Langacker notes, "[a] highly specific expression describes a situation in fine-grained detail, with high resolution" (ibid.). The opposite of specificity is schematicity, and so *relative* is schematic with respect to *aunt. Aunt*, then, serves as an instance of *relative*, for schematic terms tend to be instantiated by a number of detailed concepts. These, in turn, can elaborate coarse-grained specifications of the given schematic characterisation. Such an elaborate relationship is marked with a solid arrow: A > B, which points out different kinds of hierarchies, some of them being taxonomies. Let us have a look at a few of Langacker's (2008: 56) examples:

a)

rodent ⟶ *rat* ⟶ *large brown rat* ⟶ *large brown rat with halitisis*

b)

hot ⟶ *in the 90s* ⟶ *about 95 degrees* ⟶ *exactly 95,2 degrees*

c)

thing ⟶ *object* ⟶ *tool* ⟶ *hammer* ⟶ *claw hammer*

d)

Something happened. ⟶ *A person perceived a rodent.* ⟶ *A girl saw a porcupine.* ⟶ *An alert little girl wearing glasses caught a brief glimpse of a ferocious porcupine with sharp quills.*

Schematicity, as evident from the above linguistic data, is a fundamental element of cognition. Thanks to its role to reinforce something inherent in a great deal of mental experiences, a schema can serve as a categorising function.

2.4.4.2 Focusing

Focusing, according to Langacker (2008: 57), is another process present during the construction of a conceptual structure. Focusing is always a matter of degree, since our attention can be focused on different elements, with a different degree or can be changed altogether. As Langacker states, a lexical item provides access to a range of cognitive domains (the domain matrix) that organise its meaning. These, in turn, are ranked for centrality, and associated with their likelihood of activation. Therefore, those domains that become more accessible at a given time are foregrounded, in contrast to the ones which stay dormant in the peripheries. At the same time, focusing shows us how a lexical item is understood by an individual speaker in a given context of its usage.

The most prominent type of focusing is the foreground-background organisation, frequently referred to as figure-ground organisation, originally deriving from perceptual attention. To be more precise, those aspects of a visual scene that stand out (i.e. are undoubtedly prominent) are the foreground/figure against the (back)ground. As Taylor (2002: 10) emphasises, figure-ground organisation

> is in principle rather flexible. Often, we can reverse our figure-ground perception, making the erstwhile ground the object of attention, and can organize a scene in terms of different figure-ground alignments, by selectively focusing attention on different aspects of a scene.

However, as proved by both linguists, the phenomenon in question applies not only to matters of visual perception. Neither does it refer solely to other kinds of sensory perception. It needs to be emphasised at this point that, being context-dependent, figure-ground organisation is a crucial element in our cognition, as it manifests how a particular lexical item is understood by an individual.

Langacker (2008: 58) proposes that a possible manifestation of figure-ground alignment is categorisation, which suggests that the observed/categorised structure functions as the foreground, the background being the categorising structure. Another example provided by him is the case "where one conception precedes and in some way facilitates the emergence of another" (ibid.). Consequently, the understanding of an expression requires background knowledge on the part of the interlocutor, very often cultural in character. Hence, a sentence like *I want you to put the canned tomatoes on the top shelf of the pantry* can be misunderstood without proper cultural background knowledge. Cultural knowledge operates in tandem here with the basic knowledge deriving from our experience of the physical world, necessary to serve as the background for the proper interpretation of the sentence. Otherwise, without that background, one might think that, first of all tomatoes should be removed from the cans and, later on, placed on the shelf.

2.4.4.3 Prominence

Prominence or salience is, as Langacker (2008: 66) defines it, focusing attention on certain kinds of asymmetries displayed by language structures. Prominence has several dimensions, as a foreground may be more prominent than its background, or, within a category, the prototype can be more salient than its various extensions. This could be explained by the fact that "[w]hen we look at an object in our environment, we single it out as a perceptually prominent figure standing out from the ground. The same principle of prominence is valid in the structure of language" (Ungerer and Schmid 1996: 156). Let us deal with two kinds of prominence, that is profile-base organisation and the trajector/landmark alignment.

The part of the semantic structure of an expression that is identified as its maximal scope in all domains of its matrix is called the base, which, not being in focus, is necessary to understand the foregrounded part of the expression's conceptual content. In other words, it serves as the locus of viewing attention. In turn, the structure that is within this onstage region is called the profile. Importantly, "[t]he semantic value of an expression resides in neither the base not the profile alone, but only in their combination" (Langacker 1987: 183). However, what seems to distinguish profile-base organisation from the one of figure and ground is that the same base can provide different profiles. Langacker (2008:

66–67) gives the example of *elbow* and *hand*, which can be viewed as different profiles of one and the same base:

> In fact, it is quite common that two or more expressions evoke the same conceptual content yet differ in meaning by virtue of profiling different substructures within this common base. For instance, *Monday, Tuesday, Wednesday*, etc. all evoke as their base the conception of a seven-day cycle constituting a week, within which they profile different segments (ibid., p. 67).

However, it is fair to say that, apart from profiling a thing, an expression can also profile a relationship, as can be seen in Fig. 18, after Evans and Green (2006: 239).

Fig. 18. Familial network in which uncle *is profiled (based on Langacker (1987: 185).*

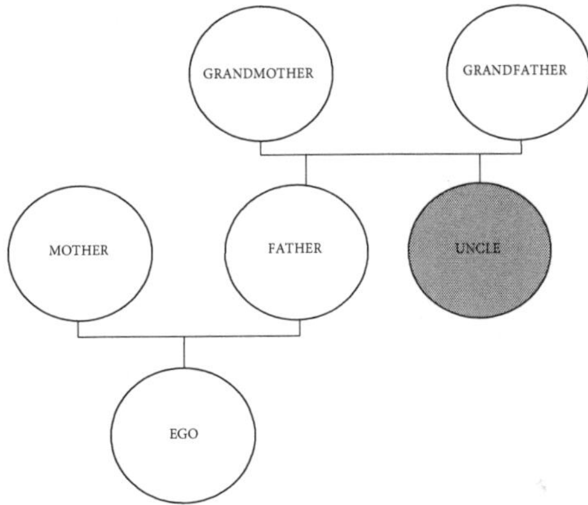

The essential content of the kin term *uncle* is the kinship relation between a male and the reference individual, referred to as *ego* by Langacker (1987: 185). The word *uncle* profiles an entity with a range of domains, that is a matrix. It includes, among others, the domains of GENEALOGY […], PERSON […], GENDER […], SEXUAL INTERCOURSE […], BIRTH […], LIFE CYCLE […], PARENT/CHILD RELATIONSHIP […], SIBLING RELATIONSHIP […] and EGO […]. The base for the conceptual category *uncle* is the network of FAMILY RELATIONS […]. It is against this base that *uncle* profiles an entity of the conceptual content of the expression's meaning. The entity is related to the *ego* due to being a MALE SIBLING of *ego*'s mother or father. What is more, it should be pointed out that "the profile is not defined as the most important or distinctive content, but rather as the entity an expression designates, i.e. its referent within the content evoked" (Langacker 2008: 67).

In the case of two verbs, *come* and *arrive,* they can both serve as a good instantiation of profile-base organisation, as seen in Fig. 19. The base for them both is

the conception of a thing (represented as a circle) moving along a special path
(represented with an arrow) to an end location (LOC).

Fig. 19. Profile-base organisation of the verbs come *and* arrive.

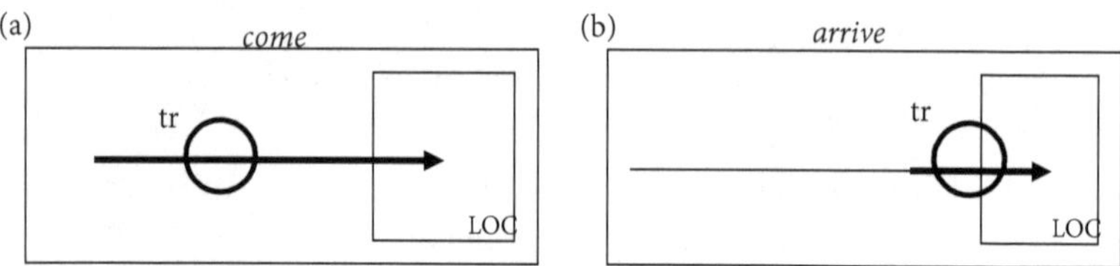

Both verbs evoke a relationship between the mover and the positions defining
the path. However, while *come* profiles the whole activity of moving, taking into
account the whole path, what *arrive* profiles is only one segment of the movement: the one when the mover finally reaches the destination.

The trajector/landmark alignment applies to expressions that, despite having
the same conceptual base and profiling the same relationship within it, have different meanings (Langacker 2008: 70–73). In this case, the entity that is evaluated
or described, that is the most prominent participant, is called the trajector (tr).
The other participant, a secondary focus, is given the name of landmark (lm).

As for an example of trajector/landmark alignment, Langacker (2008: 71) suggests the relationship between two prepositions of place: *above* and *below*. This
is owing to the fact that both indicate the relative spatial location of two things.
In addition, they profile the same relationship, for *X above Y* equals *Y below X*.
However, they are semantically different in the degree of prominence, for we use
the relationship *X above Y* to define the location of X, and *Y below X* to specify
the location of Y. The trajector/landmark alignment of the prepositions *above*
and *below* is illustrated in Fig. 20.

Fig. 20. The trajector/landmark alignment of the prepositions above *and* below.

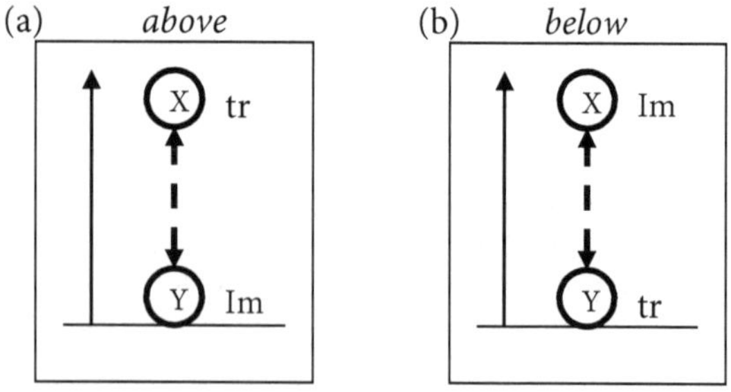

Another example of trajector/landmark alignment is the pair of expressions *have a parent* and *have a child*. First, they have the same conceptual base. Second, they profile the same relationship. Third, they are semantically distinct owing to their opposite trajector/landmark alignment. The reason is that *have a parent* is a description of a child, whereas *have a child* is a description of a parent. The relationship is shown in Fig. 21.

Fig. 21. The trajector/landmark alignment of the expressions have a parent *and* have a child.

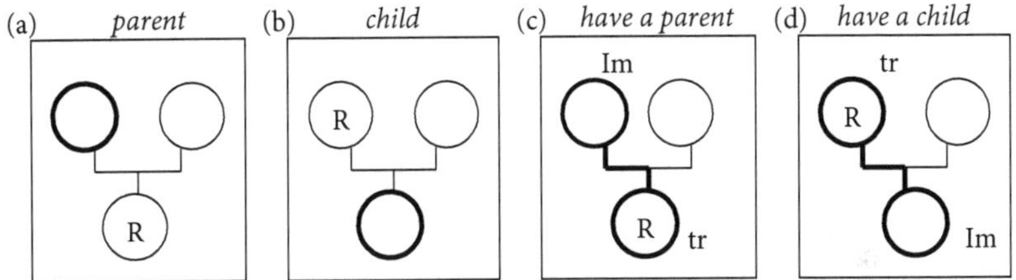

2.5 From diachrony to panchrony

The discussion in Chapter 1 led us to the conclusion that diachrony is nothing but a description of language past, a way to show the developmental paths of words. However, the question which arises in connection with this is whether such a description is enough to comprehend the mechanisms behind the phenomenon of language change? Does it give us the whole picture, letting us understand the past of (a) language? Another question arises at this juncture, namely: what makes us understand things? What makes it possible for the human mind to comprehend language and the surrounding world? It will probably be agreed that we want to achieve explanation, not description, as the key to talking about language past and language development. After all, let us recall that "there is nothing that has been created without some reason, even if human nature is incapable of knowing precisely the reason for them all" (John Chrysostom 1986, living c. 349–407). Having a look at Langacker's (1987, 1988, 1990, 1991, 1994, 1998, 1999, 2002, 2008, 2009, 2011a, 2011b, 2015) understanding of language, there are good reasons to assume that language is motivated, and the motivating factor in language change is hence the correlation of language with our living environment, everyday experience, culture, thinking or – in technical terms – conceptualisation. If so, descriptive diachrony should give way to explanatory panchrony, as understood by Łozowski (1993, 1999, 2000, 2005, 2008, 2010, 2011, 2012a, 2012b, 2012c, 2014) as "a perspective of binding past and present, of continuation, and of homogenity" (Łozowski 2008: 9), since panchrony is "a property of the human mind that, among other things, uses language". Panchrony should "be identified with what binds synchrony and diachrony" (ibid., 10). In other words, panchrony is about language change being "motivated by the speaker's changing subjectivity, the subjectivity verbalized in a never-ending process of externalizing categorization tensions" (ibid., 10). In fact, the world itself does not have meaning *per se*, but it acquires meaning through the processes of cognition that take place in the human mind. Furthermore, meaning is not a property of individual words or sentences,

> nor simply a matter of their interpretation relative to the external world. Instead, meaning arises from a dynamic process of meaning construction, which we [the authors] call conceptualization. (Evans and Green 2006: 363)

Similarly, to quote Radden, Köpcke, Berg, and Siemund (2007:1):

> meaning does not reside in linguistic units but is constructed in the minds of the language users. For the listener this means that he takes linguistic units as prompts and constructs from them a meaningful conceptual representation (…). For example, the moon is not in itself meaningful but it may be made purposeful in very different ways: astronomers and lovers have fairly disparate views of the moon.

Hence, not only is meaning constructed by the human mind, but it can also differ depending on how that minds perceives and conceives of the reality that produces, the stimuli for it to perceive. This is due to the fact that owing to different experience of language users, one word can have a few meanings ascribed, or one word can evoke different, yet usually related, concepts. In the words of Dirven and Verspoor (2004: 14), "(…) different people may categorize the same thing in the world differently and even the same person may do so at different times".

Let us take an example. As Żyśko and Żyśko (in preparation) note, the term *grasshopper*[30] 'a name for orthopterous insects of the families Acridiidæ and Locustidæ, remarkable for their powers of leaping, and the chirping sound produced by the males' (*OED*) is a compound noun coming from the noun *grass* 'plant with thin leaves that covers the ground in fields and gardens' and the verb *hop* 'to move by jumping'. Etymological sources prove that the term was first recorded in the English language in the 15th century. The question that arises in this connection is the following: what motivated the name of the insect?

One might speculate that scientific knowledge was not really rich in the 15th century, when the term first appeared in English. Hence, it must have been the emotions, the worldview of the contemporaneous inhabitants of England that

---

30 The motivation of the lexical item *grasshopper* is also analysed by Kowalewski (2016).

motivated the rise of the name for the insect concerned. Referring to Tokarski's (1993) theory of naive (cultural) models, one might suppose that in the eyes of the English people of the 15th century the insect had the feature of jumping in the grass, which appeared to be salient enough to become the base for creation of the name *grasshopper*. After all, the insects' hind femora are typically long and strong, suitable for leaping. To conclude, the English *grasshopper* is one that leaps in the grass.

The name of the Spanish equivalent of the English *grasshopper*, i.e. *saltamontes*, suggests that the features highlighted by the inhabitants of Spain are quite different. The compound noun derives from the verb *saltar* 'to jump' and the noun *monte* 'a mount'. The possible reason for such a name is that the insect jumps hills. Thus, the Spanish *saltamontes* is the one that leaps over the hills. It is interesting to note that speakers of Polish must have noticed somewhat different features of this insect, and called it *konik polny* 'little field horse'. All in all, the English, Spanish and Polish names for *grasshopper* seem to reflect subjective associations of the past generations about the real world, associations based on salient and relevant features of real-world phenomena.

Following on from Łozowski (2008: 11), language tells us much about its speakers, much more than the speakers realise it does. As we can conclude, language is a symbol of human experience. What this means is that there is a non-arbitrary relationship between linguistic form and linguistic substance. This is due to the fact that, as Łozowski (ibid.) explains, "following the implications of the Greek verb *symballo*, we attempt to relate, link, or, just literally, 'put together,' the expressions that we find in language with the experience that motivates these expressions". Hence, a symbol should be understood as "a form-substance pairing organised by the cognitively-motivated association between language and experience, with language representing (standing for) and evoking experience" (ibid.). This view follows Langacker's proposal that "language is symbolic in nature" (Langacker 2008: 1–3). In functionalist terms, language is not determinant of the human world, but a derivative of cognitive and environmental factors, and hence subordinate in relation to human experience. In other words, in order to express their conceptualisations, speakers are driven "by their predisposition to relate, metaphorically or metonymically, various experiences to one another" (Łozowski 2008: 14). This makes it possible to ascribe a panchronic dimension to language, bearing in mind the fact that in order to express oneself, one needs to disclose their changing subjectivities against the constantly changing on-line categorisation continuum. Hence, if we ask about the mechanisms behind the continuity of language change, we might propose the answer that

> [o]n our panchronic account, what facilitates the cross-generational flow of change is the human universal predisposition towards expressing experience in terms of well-defined cognitive strategies (e.g., identifying substance in form) and inferences (e.g., concrete>abstract) (Łozowski 2008:15).

In sum, dealing with functionalism, or, in other words, with a non-autonomous postulate for language, three functionally-oriented claims can be mentioned with respect to language in general and language change in particular: 1) the existence of motivated symbols over arbitrary systems, 2) the primacy of expression over communication, and 3) the advantage of function over structure. Such seems to be the general framework that is suggested by Langacker and Łozowski, the two major authors that I have followed in my approach to the issue.

2.6 Panchrony as a functional equivalent to diachrony

Panchrony is a complex issue, which cannot be disambiguated without us relating to synchrony and diachrony (Heine *et al.* 1991: 249). The relationship between synchrony and diachrony is traditionally captured in terms of opposition:

> [t]his difference in nature between chronological succession and simultaneous coexistence, between facts affecting parts and facts affecting the whole, makes it impossible to include both as subject matter of one and the same science (Saussure 1983: 101).

Hence, as can be concluded from the quotation above, synchrony and diachrony do not operate in tandem, but rather against each other. This structurally-oriented approach makes it difficult to understand why and how language changes. At the same time,

> variation and fuzziness which so many linguists tried to ignore are quite often indications that changes are in progress. This insight is not, of course, entirely new, and the observation that changes involve periods of fluctuation occurs in several places in the literature (Aitchison 1995: 38).

The statement above suggests that without the functional/cognitive/panchronic background, language change could only be described, but not explained.

Hence, we need to define panchrony. Grygiel (2012: 96) points out that panchrony is not an "invention" of cognitivism, yet it is cognitivism that gives it a new shape and view of language. For Croft (2006:72), panchrony is nothing but a "simple integration of synchrony and diachrony". If so, then panchrony is not given much independence. Its function in linguistics is to join the study of space (synchrony) with the study of time (diachrony). According to Łozowski (2008: 46), such an understanding of panchrony is like "a central strip squeezed in-between the two carriageways of a motorway, rather than an independent motorway itself". For Pain (2014: 1), "[t]he panchronic program is based on an inductive method aiming at analyzing a comprehensive set of diachronic and synchronic data as well as their socio-cultural conditions of attestation". Furthermore, Pain (2014: 4) maintains that panchrony has a *diahoric* character, as it moves through (*dia*) the boundaries (*hóros*) of others disciplines. To be more precise, a panchronician needs to examine the sociological, ethic, political, historical, and cultural environment in which a linguistics fact takes place.

The functionalist approach to language solves two fundamental problems with panchrony: 1) the link between synchrony and diachrony must not be treated in a way in which the synchronic system has priority over diachronic change, and 2) the distinction between the two cannot be one that is all or nothing. Łozowski (2008: 50) states that the functional response to the first problem is vagueness and/or fuzziness, and the one to the second problem is panchrony itself. Hence, panchrony, according to Łozowski, is "the resulting intersection of the synchronic and diachronic sets" (ibid.).

Language surely functions in time and space. After all, the relationship of language to spatiotemporal reality is seen in a multitude of levels. First of all, language reflects this reality in its semantics. Secondly, language makes it possible to transform space and time due to its symbolic character, which results in what is known as the linguistic worldview (cf. e.g. Głaz, Danaher and Łozowski 2013). Last but not least, there is an intransitive relationship between time and space, and between language. This is due to the fact that language is a function of cognition, but the latter is *not* a function of time and space. In our understanding, following Łozowski (2008: 79), although language functions in time and space, it is not these two that panchrony depends not on, but what is taken into consideration are cognitive factors. Hence, panchrony is "a way of thinking of language in terms of experiential, relative, and subjective projections", "a multi-directional progression of a non-discrete categorization process in language" (Łozowski, ibid.). In other words, what is panchronic in language is the assumption that language is a cognitive tool of human categorisation. Hence, one can say that panchrony is "language change set in the context of the evolution of human understanding" or "panchrony = language change + cognition" (Łozowski, ibid.). From this we can finally go on to set the demarcation line between diachrony and panchrony. While both of them are language change-oriented and are rooted in spatiotemporal realia, it needs to be underlined that diachrony motivates language change historically, whereas panchrony seeks for this motivation in cognition. What is more, the space-time continuum is a language variable in diachrony, but in panchrony it becomes a derivative of cognition.

As mentioned in the introduction, Łozowski's (1993, 1999, 2000, 2005, 2008, 2010, 2011, 2012a, 2012b, 2012c, 2014) understanding of panchrony goes hand in hand with Langacker's (1987, 1988, 1990, 1991, 1994, 1998, 1999, 2002, 2008, 2009, 2011a, 2011b, 2015) philosophy of language. After all, for Łozowski (2012a: 41), language is perceived as a flexible system of words that are "(…) symbols of human experience" and which, due to the influence of culture, history, other extra-linguistic factors, and primarily cognition, tend to change their meanings. To quote Łozowski (ibid.), "(…) there is always a reason, a cause, a rationale, and, thus, an explanation why a given word has come to stand for a given meaning". Hence, it is the cognitive apparatus as developed by Langacker (ibid.) that explains rather than describes the reasons for the development of meanings of words, these being influenced by changing life. After all, "[l]anguage changes (…) proportionately to changes in human understanding, it records human thinking, and words are given the meanings that represent the associations that people find appropriate" (Łozowski 2012a: 42). It is evident that Łozowski's (ibid.) panchrony was born within cognitive linguistics as understood by Langacker (ibid.), cognitive linguistics giving the answer for semantic change.

2.7 Conclusion

To conclude, the aim of Chapter 2 was to show that it is cognitive linguistics according to Ronald Langacker (ibid.) that explains the processes happening in language, semantic change being one of them. Therefore, Chapter 2 focused on the importance of functionalism, conceptualisation, symbolism, embodiment, interactionism and localisation in the philosophy of language. Furthermore, I discussed the major principles of cognitive linguistics, i.e the issue of categorisation, construal and cognitive domains, the latter ones being treated as the way that vocabulary is organised together on the basis of human experience, not on rigid lexical relationships. After all, "language is assumed to reflect certain fundamental properties and design of the human mind" (Evans and Green 2006: 5). In fact, it is according to the principles of cognitive linguistics that

> language reflects patterns of thought. (…) Language offers a window into cognitive function, providing insights into the nature, structure and organisation of thoughts and ideas (ibid.).

As has been shown, the philosophy of cognitive linguistics is crucial to the understanding of panchrony as language change plus cognition (Łozowski, ibid.). In the words of Łozowski (2012: 43), the very names *functional* and *cognitive* are meant to highlight the supposition that language is shaped by the functions people ascribe to language, of which the most important is that language expresses human cognition, experience, or, most generally, culture.

Because it is our cognition that governs and shapes the human understanding of the world, words change their meanings because we, people, change our cognition, experience, and hence associations with already existing words. In other words, cognition is the key factor leading to the process of semantic change of words.

To round off this chapter and build a bridge to the next one, I believe it is cognitive domains, not structural semantic fields, that should be treated as the motivating force behind bringing together different senses of a word and the senses of different words. In order to see how these cognitive entities group vocabulary, let us turn now to a historical semantic analysis of the English 'joyful' terminology in Chapter 3. Here, the panchrony of lexical items meaning 'joy' i.e. *bliss, cheer, delight, dream, game, gladness, glee, joy* and *mirth* is shown. The semantic evolution of the lexical items concerned is presented, taking into account the cognitive factors that govern the human mind.

Chapter 3: Panchrony and English 'Joy' Vocabulary

3.1 Introduction

The conclusions drawn from the previous chapter lead me to present the role of cognitive domains as the motivating parameters behind not only linking a word's senses together, but also senses of different words. In this chapter I would like to deal with those 'joy' vocabulary items that, having entered the English language either in the Old, Middle or Modern English periods, have survived until the present day. Therefore, I will be analysing the paths of the semantic evolution of *bliss, cheer, delight, dream, game, gladness, glee, joy* and *mirth*, and will check if all of them have retained the sense of 'joy'.

In the view of cognitive linguistics, the aim of this chapter is not only to deal with joy as an emotion, and to show the historical semantics of English 'joy' vocabulary, but also, or even more so, to seek the motivating mechanisms behind the semantic developments of the lexical items concerned. To be more specific, the analysis of the semantic evolution of English 'joy' lexical items is done within the spirit of Langacker's understanding of cognitive linguistics, as well as Łozowski's theory of panchrony. Hence, the aim of this book is to show the cognitive mechanisms of the historical semantic change of the English lexical items denoting 'joy'. The study of English 'joy' terminology was started by Fabiszak (2001); however, my aim is to extend the analysis to cognition and panchrony. As Fabiszak (2001: 39) claims,

> [w]ith historical changes in the economic and social structure of a society, the nature of relations between people and the hierarchy of values they recognise (…) undergo a change. The change in socially approved values and roles available to community members influences the perception, apprehension and cognitive structure of emotional scripts.

In order to account for the driving force behind the sense alterations of *bliss, cheer, delight, dream, game, gladness, glee, joy* and *mirth*, I will search for the conceptual domains that can be applied on two semantic levels of the aforementioned lexical items. First, we need to find a conceptual domain that is common to all senses of each individual word. Second, all the words concerned should ideally be shown to be characterised within one conceptual domain, which semantically binds them together.

3.2 The concept of 'joy' as an emotion

The constant quest for happiness, joy or gladness seems to have dominated human life to such an extent that admitting that one does not feel happy or joyful is perceived as a life failure. Markets are flooded with practical guides which tell us what to do to obtain and maintain the joy of life. One of the authors of such guides writes:

> [m]odern society is always telling us how we should be and what we should have: the right job, the right lifestyle, an acceptable body image, and so on. Don't let anyone tell you what you should be. Be your own person. Happiness is an individual thing, so do what makes you happy, but obviously not to the detriment of others. The fundamental choices as to how you live your life are your own. (George 2006: 19)

Thus, the notions of happiness and joy change. Joy ceases to be sought in good deeds, romantic love and prayer, as it was in the past, but starts to be associated with a career and good looks. However, as the research conducted in this chapter shows, this kind of positive emotion does not derive only from prosperity and appearance, but is still deeply grounded in spiritual values as well. The issue of happiness and joy was already being given serious attention in ancient times, e.g. by Aristotle, who referred to them as *eudaimonia*. To be more precise, "Aristotle's analysis has shown that there is pleasure, honour and property in a happy life, but none of these things is sufficient to specify what *eudaimonia* essentially consists of" (Sihvola 2008: 14). After all, "*eudaimonia* is something we seek as an intrinsic good for the sake of itself and not for the sake of anything else" (ibid.). What is more, human beings need to be differentiated from animals. For this very reason, according to Sihvola (ibid.: 14–15), such a form of joy and happiness can be obtained due to a disposition to realise human virtues. Aristotle distinguishes two kinds of virtues: the virtues of character or moral virtues are courage, moderation, generosity and justice, whereas the virtues of the intellect are practical reason and theoretical wisdom.

Furthermore, what needs to be mentioned in the context of the study of joy and happiness is the fact that it is considered to be both timely and timeless. In the eyes of Pessi (2008: 60), the understanding of these positive emotions has been changing with time. Whilst the past studies on joy and happiness perceived these emotions to derive from good deeds and the improvement of one's moral character, the 18th century boom in industrial development triggered

> (…) the dawn of a more subjective, psychologically-based concept of human action and human life. We moved from the Socratic question "How ought I to live" to the modern, and late-modern, question of "What do I really want?" From morality and the idea of being good we have moved toward individual needs and feeling good. (ibid.)

One is led to conclude that the sources of joy and happiness are individually shaped. Thus, if we ask what makes people joyful or happy, we can refer to Pessi's (2008: 66) research, who arrived at an answer through a survey. According to her respondents, the citizens of Finland, the most central elements that give joy and happiness are: family, health, love, friends, secure income, getting help if in need, hobbies and free time.

However, emotions viewed from the psychological perspective are represented as cognitive models, having an assertoric (fact-stating) logical structure. The assertoric structure of emotions is highlighted by Salmela (2008: 37), who says:

> Emotions are semantically and evidentially related to other states, including other emotions. They are responsive to disconfirming evidence insofar as they are not biologically pre-wired, and they evade strict contradiction. Moreover, the evaluative content of an emotion can be negated and embedded in conditional and disjunctive contexts even if the content is felt as effective only when it is asserted in an emotional experience. Therefore, the logical deep structure of joy and many other emotions is assertoric rather than expressive even if their verbal expressions are often expressive utterances. (Salmela 2008: 37)

For this reason, we can state that it is not attending a party, getting married or receiving a gift that results in the emotional response of joy, but "only an appraisal or a recognition of these events as *joyful* or *goal-conductive*, which is an underlying descriptive property of joyfulness" (ibid.: 32).

As far as expressing joy is concerned, Salmela maintains that it is our behaviour, facial expressions and other gestures, tone and pitch of voice which are the most popular ways of revealing emotions. Thus, a joyful person can express their joy by exclaiming *I feel good!*, "but she [or he] may do the same by humming her [or his] favourite tune, smiling in a relaxed way, by jumping for joy, by exclaiming "Life is wonderful""(ibid., 28) and in plenty of other ways. Thus, the forms of expressing joy can have both a verbal and a non-verbal character.

3.3 English 'joy' vocabulary: a historical semantic analysis

This section deals with the evolution of the senses of the English lexical items denoting 'joy' that have survived to the present time, and which refer to 'joy' or have 'joyful' collocations. As can be seen in the semantic research, it is the sources of joyful emotions that have pushed the words into specific directions of the development of the sense of 'joy'. The aim of the following section is to establish a matrix of conceptual domains as the tool for binding all of the senses of the presented lexemes together.

3.3.1 *Bliss*

It is commonly accepted that the etymology of the word *bliss* is linked with that of *bless*. To be more precise, both lexical items, according to <u>oed</u>, developed meanings associated with 'conferring well-being upon, making happy', especially in the religious context, God being treated as the giver of happiness. This information is also given by <u>glp</u>, for *ne seó héhste blis nis on ðám flǽsclícum lustum* 'the highest bliss is not in the fleshly lusts' but *on heofonum is singal blis* 'in heaven is eternal bliss'. The lexeme concerned already appears in the Old English period *as bliðs, bliðse,* having derived from pre-Germanic **blithiz* 'gentle, kind'. This, in turn, corresponds to ON *bliðr* 'mild, gentle', OHG *blidi* 'gay, friendly', Gothic *bleiþs* 'kind, friendly, merciful', (from <u>online ed</u>).

This religious sense of *bliss* is easily observed in the following <u>med</u> quotations, the lexeme bearing the senses:

a) 'spiritual exultation or ecstasy':

> a1150 *Homily on Vices, Virtues and Abuses in Cotton Vespasian* D.14; 18/17:[31] Spiritalis leticia, þæt is seo gastlice blisse þæt man on Gode blissige betwux unrotnysse þysser reðen wurlde.

> c.1230 *Ancrene Riwle:*[32] Leafdi seinte Marie, for þe ilke muchele blisse þet tu hefdest.

> a1475 *Ludus Coventriae;* 104/211:[33] Here body xal be so ful-fylt with blys þat she xal sone thynke þis sownde credyble.

b) 'heavenly bliss, the joys of heaven':

> c.1175 *Homilies in MS Bodley* 343; 110/22:[34] Ure murhþe, & ure wuldor, & ure blisse is on heofene.

c) 'heaven, paradise'

> c.1390 *Psalterium Beate Mariae;* 47:[35] To þe blisse þat þou art Inne. So mote we atteyne.

> a1500(1413) *The Pilgrimage of the Soul;* 5.1.86b:[36] How the soule was led up throw the heuenly speer toward the blisse.

---

31 Cf. Warner, R. D-N. (ed.) (1917; reprint 1971).
32 Cf. Tolkien, John Ronald Reuel (1962).
33 Cf. Block, Katherine S. (ed.) (1922; reprint 1961).
34 Cf. Belfour, A. O. (ed.) (1909; reprint 1988).
35 Cf. Horstmann, Carl (ed.) (1892; reprint 1987).
36 Cf. Merrel D. Clubb, Jr. (ed.) (1953).

Thus, *bliss*, being associated with the heavenly joy after death, is evidently contrasted with the pain and grief of life on Earth. This sense of *bliss*, as Oatley (2004: 99) points out, is used by the Romantic poet John Keats in his 1819 letter to his brother:

> The common cognomen of this world among the misguided and superstitious is "a vale of tears" from which we are to be redeemed by a certain arbit[r]ary interposition of God and taken to heaven – What a little circumscribe[d] straightened notion! Call the world if you Please "The Vale of Soul Making". Then you will find out the use of this world.... How then are Souls to be made? How then are these sparks which are God to have identity given them – so as ever to possess a bliss peculiar to each ones individual existence? How but by the medium of a world like this? (Oatley 2004: 99)

As a result, bliss collocates with *gastlic* 'heavenly', *eche, endeles, eterne* 'eternal', *heven* 'of heaven', and *godes* 'heavenly'. Fabiszak (2001: 44–45) mentions further collocations of *bliss*, i.e. *micel* 'much', *syngal* 'exceptional', *soðlic* 'true', *hlæfordes* 'Lord's', among others. What is more,

> [p]eople experiencing *bliss* (*brucan* 'enjoy') receive it from God (*becuman* 'get', *begitan* 'get'). God bestows it on people (*gifan* 'give', *bringan* 'bring', *gegearcian* 'prepare'), bring people to it (*gelædan*), or takes it away (*ascirian* 'separate'). People themselves can either earn it (*geearnian*) or lose it (*linnan*) through their conduct (...)". (ibid.: 45)

If one looks for more religious meanings of *bliss*, one finds the definition 'the splendour or majesty of God, divine glory', which means that these prototypical God and church going associations became profiled as the most prominent features of the word concerned, which functions as their base. As a result of this strong bond between the lexical item *bliss* and the vision of religion, God becomes a vital element of the sense of the word in question. Here, the most common collocations as given by <u>med</u> are the following: *king of bliss* 'God, Christ', *barn of bliss* 'the Christ Child', *moder of bliss* 'the Virgin Mary', *land of bliss* 'the Virgin Mary', *for godes bliss* 'by the glory of God'. The quotations below illustrate the senses of *bliss*:

> c.1175 *Homilies in MS Bodley* 343; 120/18:[37]He is soð God anes blisses, & anre mihte.

> a1225(?a1200) *Homilies in Cambridge, Trinity College* B.14.52; 115:[38] Hwat is þis blissene king [L rex glorie]?

> 1440 JOHN CAPGRAVE, *Life of Saint Norbert*; 867:[39] Þou schalt se. The blissed Trynyte rith euene in his blis.

---

37 Cf. Belfour, A. O. (ed.) (1909; reprint 1988).
38 Cf. Morris, Richard (ed.) (1873; reprint 1973).
39 Cf. Smetana, Cyril Lawrence (ed.) (1977).

It should be pointed out that *bliss* refers to the condition of being happy, living a secular life. At the same time, the word concerned stops having only religious connotations. Thus, another meaning of *bliss* is 'good fortune, prosperity, well-being', as evidenced by *med*:

> a1121 *Peterborough Chronicle*:[40] On his dæg wæs ealle blisse & ealle gode on Burh.

> a1325 (c1250) *Genesis and Exodus*; 2068:[41] Good is to dremen of win, heilnesse an blisse is ðer-in.

> a1500 *Wars of Alexander*; 1827:[42] Than suld we your blysse vnto þe berne shewe.

The Middle English sense of *bliss* can be explained by the fact that people started to realise that not only God and life with the Lord in heaven could be a source of bliss, but such an emotion could be also triggered by a number of earthly pleasures. Thus, the meaning of *bliss* extended to cover 'rejoicing, merrymaking, festivity', as well as everything that gives us joy or pleasure, which is defined by *med* as 'a source of joy, a cause of happiness; sexual gratification'. The following quotes illustrate these senses:

> a1250(?c1150) *The Proverbs of Alfred*; 96/224:[43] Wis child is fader Blisse.

> c.1390 GEOFFREY CHAUCER *Canterbury Tales: Nun's Priest's Prologue, Tale*: [44] Womman is mannes ioye and al his blis.

> a1500(?c1400) *Earl of Toulouse*; 522:[45] That oon of vs twoo Preuely to hyr goo And pray hur of hur blys.

Bearing this in mind, bliss can be, as in the first two quotations above, a child or a beloved woman, a lover. Bliss can be bodily pleasure since, as has been mentioned, sexual satisfaction has been defined this way. In other words, any joyful emotion becomes a source of bliss, since bliss covers anything pleasant that happens to a human being. Hence 'a source of joy, a cause of happiness' becomes the central sense of the lexeme concerned, and thus the schematic feature of its meaning. As Fabiszak (2001: 69–70) puts it,

> [l]iterary critics suggest that the conception of the relation between a lover and his adored lady in courtly love, as developed by the Provencal troubadours and later taken

---

40 Cf. Plummer, C. and J. Earle (eds.) (1892; reprint 1952).
41 Cf. Arngart Olaf (ed.) (1968).
42 Cf. Skeat, Walter William (ed.) (1886; reprint 1973).
43 Cf. Arngart, Olaf (ed.) (1955).
44 Cf. Manly, John M. and Edith Rickert (eds.) (1940).
45 Cf. French Walter Hoyt and Charles Brockway Hale (eds.) (1930).

up by other medieval writers, is based on the relationship between a feudal follower and his lord. However, although the lady does indeed behave like a lord, putting her knights to trials, the language used to describe the emotion between them is that of religious writings. It seems that during the period investigated the concept of 'joy' has evolved from the pre-Christian (hypothesised) OE 'joy' of a feast with other warrior-companions, organised by a powerful leader, through Christian OE and ME 'joy of heaven' offered by Christ, regarded as the king of kings, to the joy of the very earthly experience of romantic love and sexual pleasure. The final stage of the development may be either considered as a semantic weakening of the concept 'joy' or an amelioration of the concept of earthly pleasure and, in particular, love.

As for the collocations of these senses of *bliss*, we are likely to come across *bliss and bale* 'happiness and misery', *sone of bliss* 'legitimate son', *maken bliss* 'make merry', *bliss of the briddes* 'the gay singing of the birds', *angeles bliss* 'joy of angels, i.e. Virgin Mary'.

Last but not least, *bliss* is simply 'joy, happiness, pleasures', which, as <u>oed</u> evidences, has been present in the English lexicon since 971. The dates marked in the axis of time show the presence of the term *bliss* as 'joy, happiness, pleasure' in literature, as found by <u>oed</u>.

Fig. 22. The presence of the lexical item bliss *as 'joy, happiness, pleasure' in literature according to* <u>oed</u>.

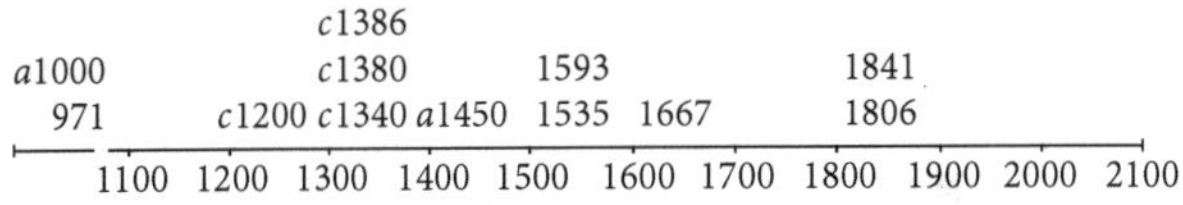

```
                        c1386
  a1000                 c1380           1593              1841
    971          c1200 c1340 a1450   1535  1667           1806
  |————————|————————|————————|————————|————————|————————|————————|————————|————————|————————|————————|
        1100     1200     1300     1400     1500     1600     1700     1800     1900     2000     2100
```

As Fabiszak (2001: 68–69) stresses, there is a certain portion of collocations that come with the two major semantic associations of *bliss*, namely 'heavenly bliss' and 'earthly bliss'. Out of the 574 instances of collocations she has analysed, dealing with such literature as *Ancrene Wisse, Shorter Poems and Caxton's Prose*, several collocating expressions come with the following frequency: *live in bliss* (2), *dwell in bliss* (1), *send to bliss* (1), *go into bliss* (1), *recover bliss* (2), *bring bliss* (4), *have bliss* (2), *perfect bliss* (1), *sovereign bliss* (1) and *heavenly bliss* (4).

Taking into account the senses of *bliss*, the matrix of domains which bind the historical semantics of the word concerned may be presented in the following way:

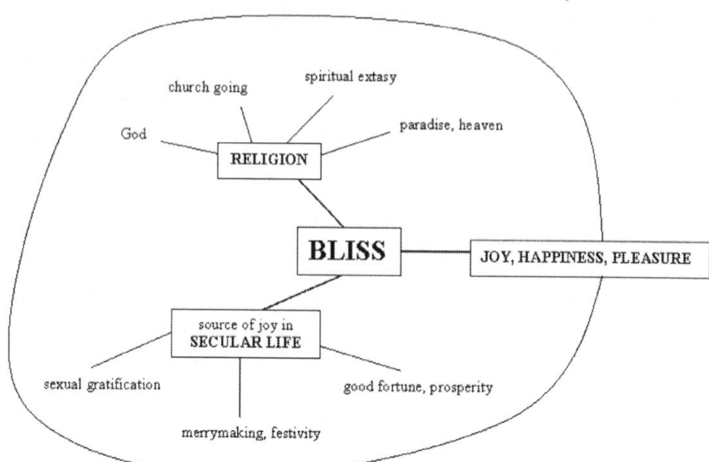

When searching for the conceptual domain that binds all the senses of *bliss*, one needs to take into account the common feature that all the senses possess. One may suppose that the domain that organises the meanings of the lexical items in question is the domain of HAPPINESS and PLEASURE. The reason for such an assumption is the fact that the previously mentioned religious experiences, i.e. spiritual exultation, the joys of heaven, paradise, and divine glory stimulate joyful emotions. So does prosperity, festivity, sexual gratification, as well as any pleasure that one can think of.

3.3.2 *Cheer*

What seems to be surprising about the lexical item *cheer* is that, as the etymological data prove, 'joy, gladness and happiness' are not its major senses. According to *LDOCE 5*, two definitions out of four refer to the state of joyful emotions. To be more precise, the meanings are: 'a shout of happiness, praise, approval or encouragement' and 'a feeling of happiness and confidence'.

Before we analyse the word's complicated development from its original sense of 'face', let us mention its etymology. *Cheer* appeared in the English language during the Middle English period in the form of *chere*. Its origin can be traced back to OF *chiere*, *chere* 'face', which corresponds to the Portuguese and Spanish *cara* 'face'. The <u>oed</u> notes that the origin of the term *cara* is uncertain. It might have developed from Greek κάρα 'head'. According to <u>oed</u>, the primary sense of the term concerned is 'face', as evidenced below:

a1225 *Ancrene Riwle*:[46] Summe iuglurs..makien cheres, & wrenchen mis hore muð, & schulen mid hore eien.

1590 SHAKESPEARE *Midsummer Night's Dream*:[47] Mids. N. III. ii. 96 All fancy sicke she is, and pale of cheere.

As the etymological source points out, this sense of *cheer* lasted in the English lexicon for four centuries, as shown in Fig. 24. The dates marked in the axis of time show the presence of the term *cheer* as 'face' in literature, as found by _oed_.

Fig. 24. The presence of the lexical item cheer as 'face' in literature according to _oed_.

<pre>
                              1483
                      1382   1475
              a1225 c1330 c1440 1590
        ├───┤
          1100 1200 1300 1400 1500 1600 1700 1800 1900 2000 2100
</pre>

However, as other etymological data suggest, the sense mentioned above also has religious connotations. According to _med_, *cheer* has also meant 'the face or presence of God'. Hence, in search for an explanation for this specialisation of the sense, one can conjecture that at the time of the Middle Ages, the face of God was attributed with some special importance. In other words, the best example, and hence the prototype, of a face was the face of God. The meaning of *cheer* 'the face or presence of God' works as an index of the principles and values of that time.

As can be seen whilst analysing the historical semantics of the terms *joy* and *bliss*, the feeling of pleasure, and joy was originally only attributed to God and contact with God. Thus, it is reasonable to claim that the church-oriented sense of *cheer* might derive from the fact that contemplating God and the paintings in churches and chapels depicting the Creator were sources of joyful emotions. Since prayer usually brings spiritual relief, a positive feeling of joy must have arisen in God's admirer. *Cheer* in the sense of 'the face or presence of God' is evidenced in the following _med_ literary contexts:

c.1384 *Wycliffite Bible*, Heb.9.24:[48] That he appere now to chere, or face, of God for vs.

a1425 (a1400) *Northern Pauline Epistles*, Cor.3.7:[49] Childre of israel myghte not loke in to þe face of hym [Moses] for..þe bryghtnesse of his chere [L uultus].

---

46 Cf. Dobson, Eric John (1972).
47 Cf. Shakespeare, William (1600).
48 Cf. Forshall, John and Frederic Madden (eds.) (1850).
49 Cf. Powell, Margaret Joyce (ed.) (1916; reprint 1973).

a1425 (c.1395) *Wycliffite Bible*, Prov.27.19:[50] As the cheris of men biholdinge schynen in watris.

Although the most common meaning of the term under consideration is 'good cheer or humour; gladness, happiness, joy', it is still used by Christians in religious contexts, especially in its verbal or adjectival form. This is noted by Charles Spurgeon, a 19th century British Particular Baptist preacher in his "Metropolitan Tabernacle Pulpit" (*spurgeongems*):

> Brothers and Sisters, the Spirit of God is not barren! If He is in you, He must and will inevitably produce His own legitimate fruit—and "the fruit of the Spirit is joy." We know this to be a fact because we, ourselves, are witnesses of it. Joy is our portion and we are cheered and comforted in the Savior.

> There is an obligation upon a Christian to be happy. Let me say it again—there is a responsibility laid upon a Christian to be cheerful!

For this very reason, it can be concluded that the aforementioned sense of *cheer* is related to the next meaning of the word, i.e. 'the face as expressing emotion, attitude or character, mien'. What is interesting to note in this context is the fact the facial expression does not necessarily have to be a happy one, as in

c.1450 *King Ponthus*:[51] She was full sory what cher so euer she made.

Thus, in order to seek parallels between the primary and the secondary meaning of *cheer*, one might conjecture that the face of God can have different expressions and, thus, His presence or contact with Him can result in the different facial expressions of His admirers. The case might be that whilst thanking God for His care, one is likely to smile and have a happy mien, whereas in the case of sorrow, asking the Lord for help, the face of the worshipper may be overwhelmed with pain. At the same time, the lexeme *cheer* underwent a widening of meaning, being present in literature for seven centuries, according to *oed*. Fig. 25 shows the dates of *cheer* as 'the face as expressing emotion, attitude or character, mien' marked in the axis of time in literature, as found by *oed*.

Fig. 25. *The presence of the lexical item* cheer *as 'the face as expressing emotion, attitude or character, mien' in literature according to* oed.

```
                    1375                 1693
          a1225 a1300 c1430   1559  1622           1830
  |________________________________________________________________|
   1100  1200  1300  1400  1500  1600  1700  1800  1900  2000  2100
```

---

50 Cf. Forshall, John and Frederic Madden (eds.) (1850).
51 Cf. Mather, Frank Jewett Jr. (1897).

The following quotes that illustrate this sense come from *med*:

c.1230 (a1200) *Ancrene Riwle*:[52] Þet ower leoue of helle nebbes beon eauer iwent somet wið luueful semblant & wið swote chere.

a1400 (a1325) *Cursor Mundi*:[53] Quat sum-euer he had in thoght, Cher mislikand made he noght.

c.1600 (c.1350) *Alexander of Macedonia*:[54] Bryght browse ibent, blisfull of chere.

The next two meanings of *cheer* as noted by *med* are 'a gesture or act indicative of an attitude or intention' and 'behaviour, manner, or an instance of it', both being the widening of the sense 'the face as expressing emotion'. Looking for the possible motivation for such a widening of meaning one might come up with the idea that it is not solely the face through which people can express their emotions. These emotions, both positive and negative, are to be found more and more frequently in body language. After all,

[w]henever we talk to or come across someone, either an acquaintance or an unknown person, we communicate with the person through numerous gestures. These gestures reflect our mental state how we are feeling or observing things. If we are not in a good mood or a little desperate, we become rather irritated and give out defensive gestures. When happy, we feel rather relaxed and active. Our mood predominantly controls most of our body gestures and signals (Sharma 2005: 9).

Reading these signals is not a difficult task. In fact, "[w]hen we are happy, we smile; when angry, we frown; when sad, we cry and tears roll down our cheeks" (ibid., 10). It could be stated that *cheer* underwent a widening of meaning from 'face' to 'gesture' and 'behaviour' since people express their emotions through their whole bodies, not only their faces.

Cheer has also meant 'state of feeling, spirit, mood, humour', thus entered the borders of the conceptual domain of EMOTIONS from the domain of BEHAVIOUR, as evidenced by *med*:

c.1300 (c.1250) *Floris and Blauncheflur*:[55] Þe Admiral chaungede his chere, For he se3 Þat eyþer wolde for oÞer [deie].

---

52 Cf. Tolkien, John Ronald Reuel (1962).
53 Cf. Morris, Richard (ed.) (1874; reprint 1961).
54 Cf. Magoun, Francis Peabody Jr. (ed.) (1929).
55 Cf. DeVries, F. C. (ed.) (1966).

a1450 *Benedictine Rule*:[56] And þat with gude cher wil fulfil What so þair souerayne tels þam vntil.

a1500 (a1450) *Generides*:[57] Be of good chere, hurt not yow to soore.

According to <u>oed</u>, the meaning concerned, being the probable source of *cheer* as meaning 'gladness, happiness, joy', died out in the 18th century:

Fig. 26. The presence of the lexical item cheer *as 'state of feeling, spirit, mood, humour' in literature according to* <u>oed</u>.

```
              c1374        1598 1667 1783-
              a1300        c1500 c1600   94
  |___________________________________________________________|
   1100  1200  1300  1400  1500  1600  1700  1800  1900  2000  2100
```

When we look at this meaning i.e. 'good cheer or humour; gladness, happiness, joy', we can state that this sort of semantic alteration is a case of narrowing. The dates marked in the axis of time in Fig. 27 show the presence of the term *cheer* as 'good cheer or humour; gladness, happiness, joy' in literature, as found by <u>oed</u>.

Fig. 27. The presence of the lexical item cheer *as 'good cheer or humor; gladness, happiness, joy' in literature according to* <u>oed</u>.

```
                              1693
                              1634
              1393 c1440 1535 1602         1842
  |___________________________________________________________|
   1100  1200  1300  1400  1500  1600  1700  1800  1900  2000  2100
```

Having first appeared in the 14th century, the meaning is traceable in the following literary quotations collected by <u>oed</u>:

1393 JOHN GOWER *Confessio amantis*:[58] This blinde boteler [i.e. Cupid] Yiveth of the trouble in stede of chere And eke the chere in stede of trouble.

1535 *Biblia*:[59] Myrth and chere was gone out of y[e] felde & vynyardes.

1842 ALFRED TENNYSON *Two Voices*:[60] Naked I go, and void of cheer.

In order to account for the possible motivation of the aforementioned "cheerful" semantic change, one can refer to the philosophical doctrines that were formed

---

56 Cf. Kock, Ernst A. (ed.) (1902; reprint 1987).
57 Cf. Wright, William Aldis (ed.) (1873, 1878; reprint as one vol. 1987).
58 Cf. Gower, John (1390).
59 Cf. Coverdale, Miles (transl.) (1535).
60 Cf. Tennyson, Alfred (1842).

110

in the period when the sense alteration under discussion took place. To be more precise, the Renaissance spirit presupposed the celebration of life as the most essential aspect of human existence. In fact,

> Renaissance people [discovered] that the world (...) was a scene of such winsome delight and astonishing beauty that God himself was surely present in it and could be worshipped in it. The affirmation and exuberant enjoyment of life on earth dissipated some quarters of the Middle Ages (Thompson 1996: 4).

Therefore, bearing in mind that the Renaissance was characterised by an omnipresent joy of life, one might be tempted to deduce that there could be two alternative explanations for the rise of the new meaning of *cheer*, i.e. 'gladness, happiness, joy'. The first possible reason for the sense shift is that many gestures, attitudes, as well as behaviours under the term *cheer* were results of pure joy or other similar joyful emotions. Thus, the term became conceptually associated with these positive emotions to such an extent that the emotions themselves were given the name of *cheer*. Another possible motivating factor behind the change is the association of 'the face' or 'the face or presence of God' with gladness, happiness and joy, and the abandonment of the ascetic life. Consequently, *cheer* was given a new meaning. However, as noted by Fabiszak (2001: 73), *cheer* in the sense 'joy' has very few occurrences:

> In 72 occurrences in Gower's *Confessio Amantis* it appears only twice with the sense of 'joy', collocating once with *lose*.[61] Out of 49 occurrences in *The Canterbury Tales*, *cheer* has the meaning of 'joy' only 3 times, the emotion here resulting from feasting, dancing, and a lovers' reunion. In the *Romaunt of the Rose* (22 occurrences), *Legend of Good omen* (16) and *Troilus and Criseyde* (26) *cheer* in the sense of 'joy' appears three times and collocates with *great, comfort* and *love*.

It can be assumed that the positive feelings of joy became most prominent in the meaning of *cheer* in the context of feasting, dancing, love and comfort. Looking at the direction of *cheer*'s semantic evolution, as presented by Fabiszak (2001: 72) in the following way:

face – facial expression – gesture – behaviour state of mind (emotion) – joy we can assume that the binding domain for all of the term's senses is the domain of EMOTION and GLADNESS. This is due to the fact that emotion (state of mind) is encoded in the human body, either in the face or in movement. Thus, emotions

---

61 While comparing happiness metaphors in English and Chinese, Chen (2010: 173) notices that *cheer* is a term employed to create metaphors denoting emotions felt in the heart. Thus, in Chinese he finds an expression that can be translated into English as to *cheer the cockles of one's heart*.

can be read from faces, facial expressions, gestures and behaviour. If a person's body language reveals a positive state of mind, the emotion becomes identified as joy and gladness. The matrix of domains engaged in the historical semantics of *cheer* is presented in Fig. 28.

Fig. 28. The matrix of domains involved in the historical semantics of cheer.

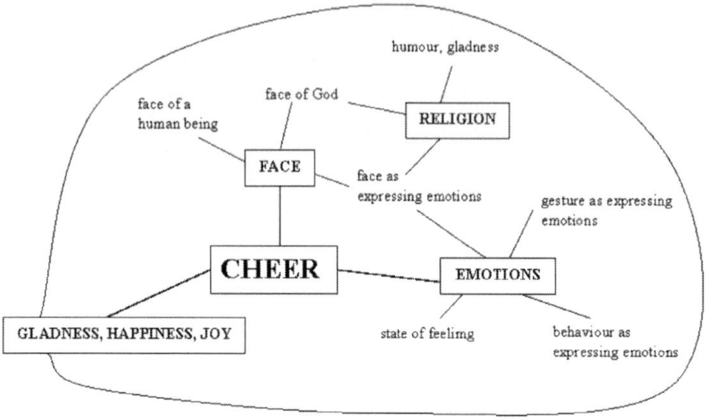

3.3.3 *Delight*

Having examined the historical development of the term *delight*, Fabiszak (2001: 73–75) notes that it is definitely related to a variety of earthly pleasures,[62] especially those associated with sexual desire. This is due to the fact that

> delight does not arise from an unexpected event like somebody's return, a riot, or good news, but results from rather conscious choices made by the experiencer, who can perform actions which lead directly and immediately to *delight* (ibid.: 74).

Consequently, *delight* becomes contrasted with reason, being on many occasions stronger than the latter.[63] Since 'an emotion of pleasure, especially sensuous delight; sexual gratification' is the primary sense of the lexeme under consideration, the Middle English form *delit(e)* can be *fleshli* and *foul*, both adjectives meaning 'bodily', and having sexual connotations, as in these quotations:

---

62 Fabiszak (2000: 306) notes that there is no collocation of *delight* and *heaven*. Thus, *heavenly delight* does not exist.

63 Wierzbicka (1992: 568) says that this could explain why *delight* cannot be associated with heaven. For her, "*delighted* appears to imply a lack of control (...), and consequently to be inconsistent with God's omnipotence".

112

c.1390 GEOFFREY CHAUCER *Canterbury Tales: Parson's Prologue and Tale*:[64] They take no reward in hire assemblynge but oonly to hire flesshly delit.

c.1430 (c.1386) GEOFFREY CHAUCER *Legend of Good Women*:[65] Thow ne feltest maladye, Save foul delyt which that thow callest love.

One can also *accomplishen /don/ performen delite(e)* 'have sexual intercourse', as in:

c.1390 GEOFFREY CHAUCER *Canterbury Tales: Manciple's Prologue and Tale*:[66] For men han euere a likerous appetit On lower thyng to parformen hir delit Than on hire wyues.

c.1425 (a1420) JOHN LYDGATE *Troy Book*:[67] He to a-complische his fleschely fals delite. Wrou3t euery þing to hir entent contrarie.

a1500 (c.1450) *The Prose Merlin*:[68] Whan he hadde don his delite with the quene, a-noon after she fill on slepe.

The sexual connotations of *delight* can be explained whilst tracing back its roots to OFr *delit*, which, as <u>oed</u> informs us, meant 'pleasure, delight, sexual desire'. According to this, the term was spelt *delite* yet, under the influence of *light*, *flight* and other similarly spelt words, dropped the ending -*e*. We can state that the joy of the body and/or sexual pleasure becomes the most prominent conceptualized feature of *delight*. As a result, since *delight* points to sexual satisfaction, this term becomes an index of sexual pleasure/joy/happiness.

Apart from 'bodily pleasure',[69] *delight* was also used in its wider sense, i.e. 'pleasure, joy'. The data evidenced by <u>oed</u> state that this meaning was last noted in literature in 1860. The dates marked in the axis of time in Fig. 29 show the presence of the term *delight* as 'pleasure, joy' in literature, as found by <u>oed</u>.

Fig. 29. The presence of the lexical item delight *as 'pleasure, joy' in literature according to* <u>oed</u>.

	a1240 c1386				1793		
	a1225 c1340		1559	1610	1736	1860	

1100	1200	1300	1400	1500	1600	1700	1800	1900	2000	2100

---

64 Cf. Manly, John M. and Edith Rickert (eds.) (1940).

65 Cf. Benson, Larry D. (ed.) (1987).

66 Cf. Manly, John M. and Edith Rickert (eds.) (1940).

67 Cf. Bergen, Henry (ed.) (1906, 1906, 1910; reprint as one vol. 1996).

68 Cf. Wheatley, Henry B. (ed.) (1865, 1866, 1869, 1899; reprint as two vols. 1987).

69 That delight has been inevitably associated with the body is evident. As Kivistö (2008: 96) emphasises, the Spanish scholar and humanist at the turn of the Middle and Modern English periods, Juan Luis Vives, ascribed delight very closely to frivolity and entertainment, such as staging feasts, love-making, drinking alcohol etc.

However, *LDOCE 5* still provides the sense of *delight*, mentioning such fixed expressions as *with/in delight, to somebody's delight/ to the delight of somebody, squeal, gasp, cry of delight*.

Furthermore, as it appears from the etymological source mentioned above, the 14th century witnessed the rise of a new meaning of the word under discussion, namely 'charm, delightfulness; the quality which causes delight', the presence of which over the centuries is visible in Fig. 30. The dates marked in the axis of time show the presence of the term *delight* as meaning 'charm, delightfulness; the quality which causes delight' in literature, as found by <u>oed.</u>

Fig. 30. The presence of the lexical item delight *as 'charm, delightfulness; the quality which causes delight' in literature according to* <u>oed</u>.

<pre>
                              1500- 1662
                    c1385   20 c1600   1804
        |---|----|----|----|----|----|----|----|----|----|----|
          1100 1200 1300 1400 1500 1600 1700 1800 1900 2000 2100
</pre>

This sense of *delight* can be testified in the following literary quotes:

> a1513 William Dunbar *Poems:*[70] No flour is so perfyt, So full of vertew, plesans and delyt.

> 1662 BALTHAZAR GERBIER *A Brief Discourse concerning the three chief Principles of Magnificent Building viz., solidity, conveniency, and ornament*; part 38:[71] The Louver at Paris with the delight of the annexed Tuilleries.

Therefore, the sources of delight are numerous. Fabiszak (2001: 75) points out that this sort of emotion may result from, amongst other things, singing, eating, drinking, entertainment, which confirm the bodily dimension of *delight*. Looking for the cognitive explanation of the aforementioned semantic change of the word under discussion, one can suspect that this time some other bodily pleasures, not only sexual satisfaction, became, on the grounds of embodiment, conceptually associated with the potential causes of delight, and pointed towards *delight*.

Today, the term collocates with a variety of expressions: *LDOCE 5* provides the reader with such collocations as: *it is a delight to do something, take delight in doing something, the delight of something, a yell of delight, be in a transport of delight, childlike delight, a cry of delight, culinary delights, delight in something, hug yourself with delight, sample the delights of something, shiver with delight, unholy delight, watch (somebody/something) with delight, pure delight, sheer delight, laugh of delight, cry of delight*.

---

70 Cf. Bawcutt, Priscilla (ed.) (1998).
71 Cf. Gerbier, Balthazar (1662).

All the senses of *delight* in its semantic development are visible in a matrix of domains of the word concerned in Fig. 31.

Fig. 31. The matrix of domains involved in the historical semantics of delight.

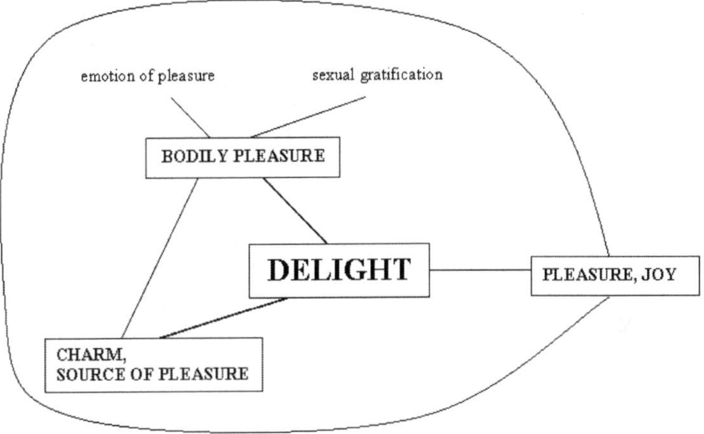

In order to account for the common conceptual domain that groups all the senses of *delight*, we may come up with the domain of PLEASURE. After all, delight in whatever form, physical or intellectual, works on the senses, bringing a feeling of pleasure.

3.3.4 *Dream*

Relying on the available etymological sources, we may state that OE *dream* is a cognate of OS *drôm* 'mirth, noise, minstrelsy'. It is interesting to note that the OE *dream* meaning 'joy, happiness' is usually differentiated from MidE/ModE *dream* 'a vision during sleeping', these two terms being treated as two separate entities in the dictionary. Although *oed* reports that "[m]uch study has failed to show that OE *dream* 'noisy merriment' is the root of the modern word for 'sleeping vision'", two stands have been taken on this issue, the homonymy hypothesis and the non-homonymy hypothesis. To quote Łozowski (2000: 90):

Although there is general consensus among the adherents of the Homonymy Hypothesis as to the double origin of the English DREAM forms (…), at least two different explanations have been offered for the actual appearance of the sense 'sleeping vision' in the 13th century. *OED* and Skeat (1882, 1884, 1898) seem to favour the possibility of the MidE DREME developing its sense from the missing OE cognate of the OS DROM 'dream'. This is based on the assumption that there were two distinct DREAM words in

OE and DROM words in OS. That it is only in the latter that both homonyms passed into the written rewords might have been because – as _OED_ explains – "the prevalence of DREAM 'joy, mirth, music', had caused DREAM 'dream' to be avoided, at least in literature, and SWEFN, lit. 'sleep' to be substituted.

Thus, according to the homonymy hypothesis, MidE dream _drém_ 'sleeping vision' is thought to have come from the Germanic root _draumo_ 'illusion', whereas OE _dréam_ 'joy' is considered to be rooted in the Greek _thrulos_ 'noise, shouting'. On the other hand, as Łozowski (2000: 91) notes, there is enough evidence to believe that _dream_ is a polysemous term. The reason for such a statement is the fact that, according to Ehrensperger (1931), not only OE _dream_ but also OS _drom_ go back to the Greek _thrulos_. Whether _dream_ 'joy' and _dream_ 'sleeping vision' are semantically convergent or not, it should be mentioned that _dream_ was first noted in English in the 9th century in the sense of 'joy, gladness, mirth, rejoicing'. The _oed_ date chart of the word is presented below:

Fig. 32. _The presence of the lexical item_ dream _as 'joy, gladness, mirth, rejoicing' in literature according to_ oed.

```
1002
 975
a830        c1205

 ┬───┬────┬────┬────┬────┬────┬────┬────┬────┬────┬
 1100 1200 1300 1400 1500 1600 1700 1800 1900 2000 2100
```

The following citations document this meaning of _dream_:

1002 _Will of Wulfric:_[72] God ælmihtig hine awende of eallum Godes dreame.

c.1205 LAYAMON _Brut:_[73] Heo æten, heo drunken: dræm

On the basis of the quotations collected by _glp_ one has good grounds to assume that the word _dream_ was usually used to refer to 'heavenly joy'. The rationale behind such an assumption is the fact that on many occasions, the term is used in a religious context, as in the following quotations:

Codex Exoniensis:[74] Ðǽr biþ engla dréam _there [in heaven] is joy of angels._

CÆDMON:[75] Heó móton ágan dreáma dréam mid Gode _they may possess joy of joys with God._

---

72 Cf. Sawyer, Peter Hayes (1979).
73 Cf. Layamon (1963–1978).
74 Cf. Thorpe, Benjamin (1842).
75 Cf. Thorpe, Benjamin (1832).

116

Dream as 'earthly joy' is also evident in literature:

Codex Exoniensis:[76] Ðǽr biþ drincendra dreám se micla *there is the great joy of drinkers.*

Saxon Chronicles:[77] Hér ge-endode eorþan dreámas Eádgár Engla cyning *in this year* [A. D. 975] *Edgar, king of the Angles, ended the pleasures of earth,* Chr. 975; Erl. 124, 29

In the eyes of cognitive linguistics, the semantic evolution of *dream* is very similar to that of *cheer*, the term being originally associated with religion and secondarily with secular life. The motivation for such a change can be found in the changing conceptualisation of the emotion of joy. We can state that *dream*, after initially profiling religion, changes the scope of the profile to cover secular pleasures instead. Hence, in terms of the idea of language functionalism, *delight* was given different meanings throughout the centuries because those meanings were functionally appropriate to the values and ideas of a particular era.

Taking into consideration the next meaning of the lexical item concerned, i.e. 'the sound of a musical instrument, especially a bell, trumpet etc.', we might ask about the possible mechanisms for the motivation behind its semantic development. The only probable reason for such a state of affairs is the fact that music, being far more popular than the written forms of communication, was treated as a medieval representation of the human body. Thus, it soon became associated with joyful emotions, triggering joy and happiness.[78] It needs to be emphasised that even nowadays the fixed expression *be music to your ears* refers to someone's words or voice when they make you happy or pleased. At the same time it should be mentioned that the sense of *dream* as 'the sound of a musical instrument' also evolved. As it turns out, a source of joy could be found not only in the sound of an instrument but also in a voice or a song. Consequently, the word *dream* could be perceived as 'voice, speaking' as well as 'singing, a song'. *Dream* as 'the sound of a musical instrument' is documented in these *med* quotations:

c.1225 *Body and Soul:*[79] Ne mostes þu iheren þeo holie dræmes, Þeo bellen rungen, [þet un]ker becnunge wæs.

---

76 Cf. Thorpe, Benjamin (1842).

77 Cf. Earle, John (ed.) (1865).

78 Note that the word *dream* started to have negative connotations, which is evident in its sense 'noise, din'.

79 Cf. Moffat, Douglas (ed.) (1987).

a1300 (a1250) *Bestiary*:[80] Ðanne remen he alle a rem, so hornes blast oðer belles drem.

a1400 *Ancrene Riwle*:[81] Hij schull on domesday arisen wiþ þe dredeful drem of þe aungels bemen.

Dream as 'voice, speaking' is clearly visible in:

c.1275 (a1216) *The Owl and the Nightingale*:[82] Ich singe efne, Mid fulle dreme & lude stefne.

c.1300 (c.1250) *Floris and Blauncheflur*:[83] To hire louerd heo sede wiþ stille dreme.

a1500 (c.1386) *Life of Saint Erkenwald*:[84] With a drery dreme he dryves owte wordes.

The meaning 'singing, a song' is represented by the following examples:

c.1300 *South English Legendary: St. Brendan*:[85] Þe foul a-3ein hem sone he drou3; þe drem of is winguene murie was.

c.1450 *Swarte smekyd*:[86] Stark strokes þei stryken on a stelyd stokke..Lus, bus! las, das! rowtyn be rowe: Swech dolful a dreme, þe deuyl it todryue!

c.1600 (c.1350) *Alexander of Macedonia*:[87] Hee chases by enchauntement þe chamber within And with a dragones drem dreew too þe bedde.

As a result, the word under discussion can be found in such word combinations as *mid dreri drém* 'mournfully, *mid fui drém* 'in full voice, loudly' *with stile dreme* 'in a low voice, softly', as well as *maken drém* 'to lament'.

Looking at Fig. 33 which shows the matrix of domains involved in the semantic evolution of *cheer*,

---

80 Cf. Hall, Joseph (ed.) (1920).

81 Cf. Zettersten, Arne (ed.) (1976).

82 Cf. Grattan, John H. G. and G. F. H. Sykes (eds.) (1935; reprint 1973).

83 Cf. DeVries, F. C. (ed.) (1966).

84 Cf. Peterson, Clifford (ed.) (1977).

85 Cf. Horstmann, Carl (ed.) (1887; reprint 1987).

86 Cf. Sisam, Kenneth (ed.) (1921; reprint 1933).

87 Cf. Magoun, Francis Peabody, Jr. (ed.) (1929).

Fig. 33. The matrix of domains involved in the historical semantics of dream.

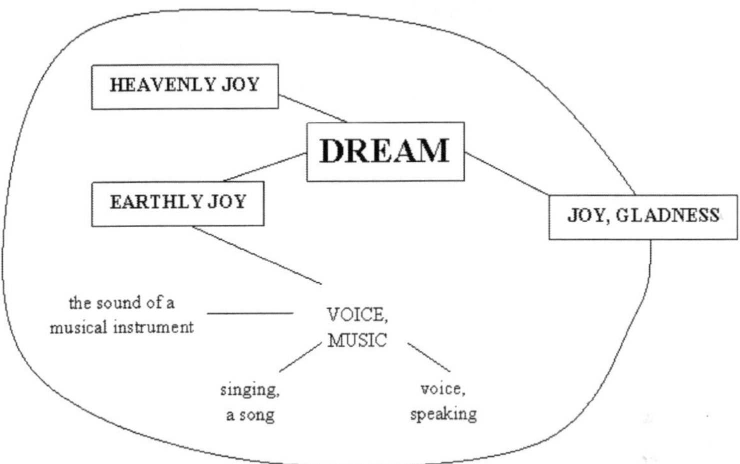

We can say that the conceptual domain that binds these senses of *dream* is the one of GLADNESS. Consider the fact that, while experiencing the feeling of joy or mirth, one starts to feel glad. What is more, listening to or hearing sounds produced by a musical instrument, someone's voice or song, can also bring up positive emotions and result in a feeling of gladness.

3.3.5 *Game*

The lexical item *game*, although nowadays mentally associated mainly with sport, appears to have developed the sense 'joy, happiness, delight, gaiety, mirth, amusement'. *Game*, the contemporary usage of which is 'amusement, pastime, diversion' as evidenced by Babcock Gove (1995), and is a common Germanic word. According to <u>online ed</u>, OE *gamen* 'game, joy, fun, amusement' corresponds with OFris *game* 'joy, glee', ON *gaman*, OHG *gaman* 'sport, merriment', Danish *gamen* and Swedish *gamman* 'merriment'. Thus, it appears that *game* can be referred to both earthly and heavenly joy. The data collected by <u>glp</u>, where OE *gamen* is defined as 'joy, pleasure, mirth, sport, pastime' include the following quotation:

> *Boethius:*[88] Næs ðæt hérlíc dæd, ðæt hine swelces gamenes gilpan lyste *that was not a glorious deed, that he should wish to boast of such sport.*

---

88 Cf. The Anglo-Saxon metrical version of the metrical portions of Boethius, with a verse translation by M. Tupper.

Moreover, _med_ mentions the existence of game as 'heavenly joy':

> a1425 (a1400) *The Siege of Jerusalem (Titus and Vespasian):*[89] God is euer þere, beþ þre oþer tweye, That beþ ygaderd to speke in his name, In his worshipp for soule game.

This sense appeared in the English language around the 11ᵗʰ century, as shown by the following _oed_ date chart. The dates marked in the axis of time show the presence of the term *game* as 'heavenly joy' in literature, as found by _oed_.

Fig. 34. The presence of the lexical item game *as 'heavenly joy' in literature according to* oed.

```
                    c1386 c1485  1588
                    1375 c1450  1580
                     13..  c1440  1560
                1297 c1340 c1430 1549-
                c1250 c1320 c1425    62
    a1000       a1200 a1300 c1400  1523              1879
    ├────┬────┬────┬────┬────┬────┬────┬────┬────┬────┤
      1100 1200 1300 1400 1500 1600 1700 1800 1900 2000 2100
```

This meaning of *game* can be documented with the _oed_ quotations below:

> a1000 *Boethius:*[90] He het him to gamene ðeara forbærnan Romana burið.

> 1375 BARBOUR *The Bruce:*[91] [Bruce] maid yaim gamyn and solace.

> c.1450 *St. Cuthbert* (Surtees):[92] 1188 Com Þe batemen with gamen and gle.

For this very reason, we can talk about *ertheli gāme* 'wordly pleasure', *fleshli gāme* 'bodily pleasure', *gastli* or *soule gāme* 'spiritual joy'. Furthermore, we can do *something in (with) game* 'with pleasure', for (one's) pleasure'. We are also likely to come across such collocations as: *game and glee, game and play, joy and game, game and solace, upon one's game* 'in fun' and *no game* 'no fun'. Similarly to other terms denoting 'joy', e.g. *bliss*, the term *game* also offered religious connotations due to the zeitgeist values of the time when it entered the English lexicon, and was also profiled with the meaning of 'heavenly joy'. Since, as can be observed from life itself, great pleasure, joy and amusement are derived from social life, this being accounted for by festivity, music, laughter, love-making and jokes, the emotions, it turns out, have become mentally associated with the term *game* to such an extent that they have eventually been categorised and lexicalised as GAME. As a

---

89 Cf. Fischer, Rudolf (1903, 1904).
90 Cf. Griffiths, Bill (ed.) (1994).
91 Cf. Barbour, John (1375).
92 Cf. Fowler, Joseph Thomas (ed.) (1891).

120

result, the term profiles the senses of 'festivity, revelry, amusement, play, music', as evidenced by the following _med_ quotations:

> c.1275 (a1200) LAYAMON *The Brut*:[93] Gleomen sculden wurchen burd..and eten heore wullen..and drinken and dreomen..þis gomen heom sculde i-lasten.

> c.1395 GEOFFREY CHAUCER *Canterbury Tales: Wife of Bath's Prologue and Tale*:[94] His wyf was at a someres game.

> a1500 (c.1340) RICHARD ROLLE *English Psalter and Commentary*:[95] Now thai haf vmgifen me in the crosse hyngand, as foles that gedirs til a somere gamen.

As a result, one can *haven gāme* 'amuse oneself', and *maken* it 'make sport; make fun'. We can also find the word in the following collocations: *gomin and gle/jolite/ pleie solas* or *joie (mirthe) and gamen*, both expressions meaning 'amusement and merrymaking'. *No game*, in turn, is 'no laughing matter'.

Game as 'love-making', especially a sexual intercourse, appeared in English in the 13th century, as visible in the following _oed_ date chart:

Fig. 35. The presence of the lexical item game *as 'love-making' in literature according to* _oed_.

```
          1297
         c1275                              1964
         c1230      c1400  1522  1606       1938
     ├─────────────────────────────────────────────┤
     1100 1200 1300 1400 1500 1600 1700 1800 1900 2000 2100
```

This sense is also easily deduced from literature (*oed*):

> 1297 *The Chronicle of Robert of Gloucester*:[96] So longe hii dude such sacrefise & pleide such game ðat hii adde an doȝter averne was hire name.

> 1522 *World & Child*:[97] I am a child gotten in game and in grete synne

> 1938 GREENE *Brighton*:[98] What mattered was the game. The two main characters made their stately progress towards the bed sheets.

'A joke or jest', another meaning developed by *game*, appeared in English also in the 13th century (_med_):

---

93 Cf. Brook, George L. and Robert F. Leslie (eds.) (1963, 1978).
94 Cf. Manly, John M. and Edith Rickert (eds.) (1940).
95 Cf. Bramley, Henry R. (ed.) (1884).
96 Cf. Wright, William Aldis (ed.) (1887).
97 Cf. Anonymous (1522).
98 Cf. Greene, Henry Graham (1938).

> c.1275 (a1200) LAYAMON *The Brut*:[99] Heore 3elp & heore gome ilomp heom seoluen to scame.

> a1500 SIR RICHARD ROS *La Belle Dame Sans Mercy*:[100] When y speke after my best avise, yet set it at nought, but make therof a game.

This word tends to produce fixed expressions connected with humour: *maken game of* 'to turn (something) into a joke', *in (on/with) game* 'in fun; jokingly', *bitwixen game and ernest* 'half in fun', *maken ernest of game* 'to take a joke seriously', *in (for) ernest or in (for) game* 'either in earnest or in jest'.

As the etymological data points out, another popular joyous activity was sport, especially those common in medieval Europe. Hence, *game* was given the meaning 'any of the sports of hunting, fishing, hawking or fowling'. Consequently, one can be *maister of the game* 'royal officer in charge of hunting' or *unto the game* 'trained' as can be seen below (*med*):

> c.1410 EDWARD PLANTAGENET *Master of Game*:[101] The which book shal be named and called Mayster of Game. I am Maister of this game wiþ þat noble prince your fadere.

> a1393 JOHN GOWER *Confessio Amantis*:[102] Thei scholden come Unto the gamen alle and some to do such maistrie as thei myhte.

Later on, since all the aforementioned sports are connected with chasing, the object of the chase itself started to be called *game*, the term having gained the new sense of 'the animal hunted' and soon being narrowed to 'wild animals'. The reason for such a sense specialisation is probably the fact that the activity of chasing was mentally associated with wild animals only. On the other hand, the meaning 'any of the sports of hunting, fishing, hawking or fowling' was broadened to 'an athletic contest, sport in which people compete with each other', this, eventually, having connotations with 'success in a contest, the prize of victory'.

From the perspective of cognitive linguistics, it seems evident what the motivation behind the semantic evolution from 'heavenly joy' to other bodily joys should be. With time, people, thinking about the causes of pleasures, started to construe them as being present in different activities outside the Church. Therefore, the conceptualisation of JOY as linked with earthly pleasures led to the fact that those earthly pleasures, e.g. 'festivity', 'love-making', 'a joke', 'a sport', 'hunting', 'success', etc. seem to be prototypical kinds/sources of *game* today. As far as the

---

99   Cf. Brook, George L. and Robert F. Leslie (eds.) (1963, 1978).
100 Cf. Furnivall, Frederick J. (ed.) (1866; re-ed. 1903; reprint 1965).
101 Cf. Baillie-Grohman, William A. and Florence Baillie-Grohman (eds.) (1904).
102 Cf. Macaulay, George C. (ed.) (1900; reprint 1978).

matrix of domains involves in the historical semantics of *game* is concerned, it is presented below:

Fig. 36. The matrix of domains involved in the historical semantics of game.

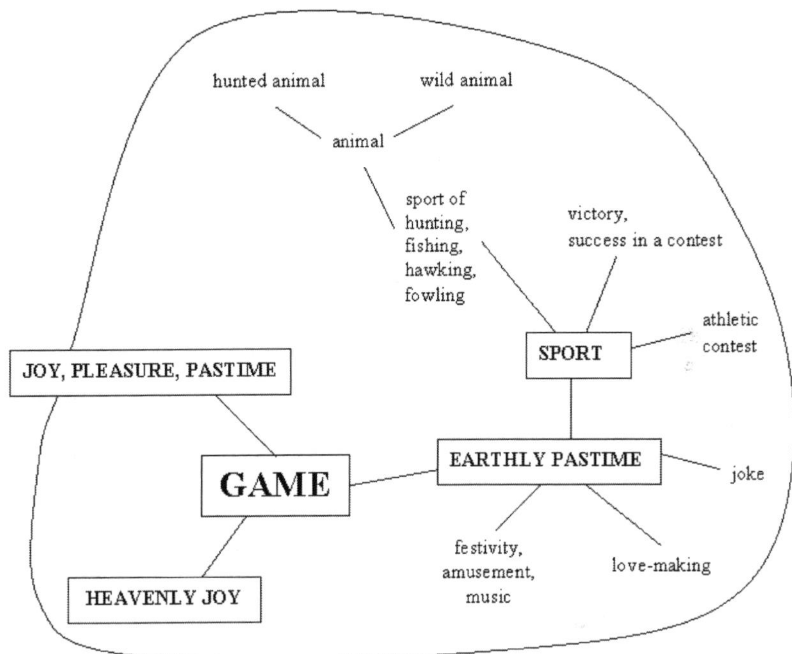

In search of the parallels between all the aforementioned meanings of *game*, one needs to pay attention to the role of the conceptual domain PLEASURE. After all, anything that is pleasant gives us joy, happiness, delight. This kind of relationship can also work in the opposite direction. In fact, any sort of joy, happiness or delight contributes to the rise of pleasant feelings. Hence, as has already been mentioned, such elements of life as festivals, music, laughter, love-making and jokes are also generally considered pleasant, and thus bringing joy. However, these activities are not the only ones that can cause pleasure. Another source of joy can be found in sport, not only in hunting, fishing etc. but sport of whatever kind of competition.

3.3.6 *Gladness*

The lexical item *gladness* is a compounded form of the adjective *glad* and the suffix *–ness*. The adjective has already appeared in the Old English period, its form being *glæd* 'cheerful, joyful, happy'. It is interesting to notice that OE *glæd* corresponds to ON *glaðr* 'bright, joyous'. However, as _oed_ notes, its origin is to be sought in OHG *glat* 'smooth', the term being the source of Ger. *glatt*, Du. *glad*, Fris. *gled*, as well as, what might be surprising, OSl. *gladŭkŭ*. A great amount of the etymological data would seem to suggest that the word concerned, having already appeared in the English language in the 10th century, had only one sense, i.e. 'the state of being glad, joy' (_oed_) and 'joy, cheerfulness' (_glp_). However, the Bosworth-Toller Anglo-Saxon Dictionary (henceforth _btasd_) lists four senses of gladness:

1) 'the state of feeling of being glad' as contrasted with *unrótness* 'sadness, sorrow, trouble, gloominess' and *asolcennys* 'idleness, sloth, laziness' as in

   > Hí gesíðodon tó Críste fram eallum costnungum tó ealre glædnysse *from all temptations to joy.*

2) 'a pleasurable condition, state of happiness', as in

   > Ealle angnysse and uneáðnysse smyltnysse and glædnesse gehátað.

3) 'alacrity, cheerful readiness' as can be seen in

   > Godes þegnas mid glædnysse efston, ástræhton heora swuran tó slæge for Críste.

4) 'kindness, gentleness, favourable consideration, favour', as in

   > His glednes *hilaritas eius* (sicut ros super herbam, ita et *hilaritas eius*).

In order to account for the conceptual domain binding all these senses together, one might be tempted to claim that such a domain is CHEERFULNESS. The reason for the possible explanation is the fact that when one feels cheerful, one is glad. What is more, having attained a state of happiness, one experiences cheerfulness. Furthermore, being cheerful or glad, one is likely to act willingly, thus readily. Last but not least, there is the ongoing correlation between being gentle, kind and cheerfulness, joy: "But the fruit of the spirit is love, joy, peace, long-suffering, kindness, goodness, faithfulness, gentleness, self-control. Against such there is no law" (*NT*, 1966: 435; Galatians 5: 22–23). Therefore, as evidenced above and analysed by Fabiszak (2001: 76), the lexeme *gladness* is used to refer to both 'heavenly joy' and 'earthly joy'. The data given by _med_ suggests that the term concerned also developed the meanings of 'delight, pleasure' and 'brightness', the former being evidenced in the following *med* literary quotations:

> a1393 JOHN GOWER *Confessio Amantis*:[103] He hadde riht a gret gladnesse Of that he bothe syh and herde.

> c.1425 (a1420) JOHN LYDGATE *Troy Book*:[104] I haue in party gret gladnes Of þi manhod.

> c.1443 REGINALD PECOCK *The Rule of Christian Religion*:[105] So þat he be not found in gladnes þat he þo synnys dide.

The latter sense is visible below:

> a1425 *Guy de Chauliac's Grande Chirurgie*:[106] Vnto þu see helþe of þe place bi resolucioun & gladnez [*Ch.(2)*: gladenesse or fairenesse; L hilaritatem] of þe skyn.

The term collocates with such verbs as *ben in* ~ 'to rejoice' *maken* ~ 'to rejoice', *ben founden in* ~ 'to be pleased', *haven* ~ 'take pleasure in doing something.'[107]

Having analysed *Confessio Amantis, The Canterbury Tales, Trailus and Criseyde, The Legend of Good Women* and *Romaunt of the Rose*, Fabiszak (2001:77) points out that there appear to be 43 occurrences of *gladness* and its corresponding *glandschipe*, and 20 occurrences of *glad*. *Gladness* turns out to be modified by such adjectives as *blissful, light* and *wonderful* and it "co-occurs with *delight* (1), *mirth* (1), *joy* (2), *play* (1) and *sweetness* (1)." She notes that the sources of gladness are numerous: music, a walk, meeting somebody dear, a lovers' reunion, love, the birth of a child, hunting and even martyrdom and another person's failure. After all,

> [s]ome [philosophers] have thought that the presence of positive feelings makes life go well, while others think that it is having one's desires fulfilled. Overall happiness has to do with both one's situation (e.g. being fortunate) and with one's state of mind (gladness etc.) (Pessi, 2008: 61)

Taking all the senses of *gladness* into account, one may assume that the conceptual domain that brings them all together is the domain of HAPPINESS/CHEERFULNESS. This is due to the fact that a pleasurable condition, cheerful readiness, kindness and gentleness, delight and pleasure or brightness do indeed make a

---

103   Cf. Macaulay, George C. (ed.) (1900; reprint 1978).
104   Cf. Bergen, Henry (ed.) (1906, 1906, 1910; reprint as one vol. 1996).
105   Cf. Greet, William C. (ed.) (1927; reprint 1987).
106   Cf. Wallner Björn (1969, 1976, 1982, 1988).
107   Fabiszak (2001: 77) notes that we can also *bathe in gladness* and *make somebody gladness (or glad)* or *do somebody gladness (or glad)* 'to please' or 'to entertain'.

person happy and/or cheerful. The matrix of domains involved in the semantic evolution of *gladness* is presented in Fig. 37.

Fig. 37. The matrix of domains involved in the historical semantics of gladness.

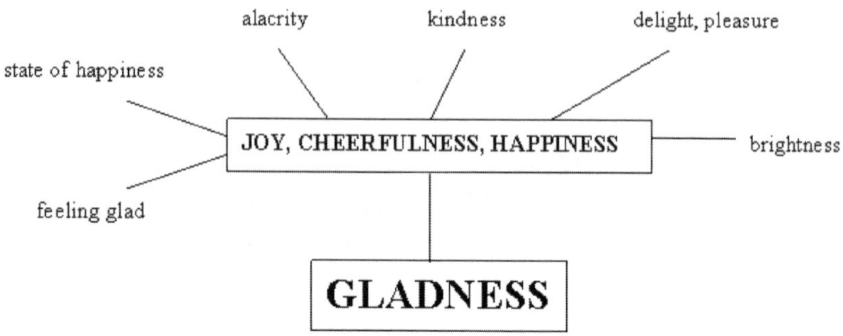

3.3.7 *Glee*

Etymological data points out that there is a link between OE *glíw, gléo* and the OE stem *gliujo-*, yielding the forms of *glíeʒ, glíʒ, glíw* and *glío*. The term, together with its Middle English form *glew* and *gle*, was likely to appear mostly in poetry, and almost died out in the 17th century. The end of the 18th century witnessed its reappearance. However, the circumstances of such a come-back remain unknown. Although the contemporary usage of *glee*, as noted by *LDOCE 5*, is 'a feeling of satisfaction and excitement, often because something bad has happened to someone else', it needs to be remembered that it has come a long way through different stages in its semantic evolution before it developed the present sense.

The oldest, and now obsolete, meaning of the word concerned is 'entertainment, play, sport'. It appeared in the English language as early as the 8th century, as can be seen in Fig. 38:

Fig. 38. The presence of the lexical item glee *as 'entertainment, play, sport' in literature according to* oed.

*a*1000	*a*1310	
*a*700	*c*1300 *c*1450 1535	

| 1100 | 1200 | 1300 | 1400 | 1500 | 1600 | 1700 | 1800 | 1900 | 2000 | 2100 |

This is evidenced by the *oed* quotations below:

a700 *The Epinal Glossary: In mimo,* in gliuuæ.

a1310 BROOK *Harley* Lyrics:[108] Mury hit ys in hyre bour, With gomenes ant with gleowes.

As can be seen, *glee* collocated with *have* and *make,* the latter collocation bearing the form of *to make oneself glee* 'to make sport' and *to make one's glee of/on* 'to make sport of (a person or thing)'. Soon the term developed the sense 'scheming, intrigue', as evident below (*med*):

a1300 *Þeo soþe luue:*[109] Yeue vs þat we moten fleo euer sunegynge, And þene feond and al his gleo and al his twyelinge.

a1400 (a1325) *Cursor Mundi:*[110] Ihon..fasted fourti dais..Þe warlau wili has him soght, Faand he wald him if he moght, For it was sene he noght him kneu, Quen he be-gan do suilk a gleu [vr. glew].

In order to explain the possible motivation mechanisms behind the aforementioned sense development, one needs to remember that intrigues and schemes were a popular form of entertainment, especially in court circles. Plots that could ruin other people's reputation were frequently heard of in the Middle Ages. Therefore, the rise of the contemporary meaning of *glee* as noted by *LDOCE 5* does not surprise. After all, on many occasions have people proved that someone else's harm or other sort of trouble has triggered another's feeling of joy, pleasure or satisfaction.

Since sport, entertainment and intrigues undoubtedly gave much joy and pleasure, these meanings of *glee* must have become mentally associated with these positive emotions to such an extent that the term itself was given the meaning of 'mirth, joy, bliss, pleasure, delight', as well as 'a source of joy'. While the former sense is documented with such *med* quotes as:

a1250 *Mon may longe:*[111] In wo sal þi wele enden, in wop þi gle.

c.1440 SIR DEGREVANT:[112] To brynge þe dere to þe grounde Was his maste glewe.

c.1475 (c.1399) *Mum and the Sothsegger:*[113] 3it forbede I no burne to be blithe sum while; But alle þinge hath tyme for to tempre glees.

the latter is evidenced by:

---

108   Cf. Brook, George L. (1968).
109   Cf. Morris, Richard (1872; reprint 1988).
110   Cf. Morris, Richard (ed.) (1874; reprint 1961).
111   Cf. Brown, Carleton (ed.) (1932).
112   Cf. Casson, Leslie F. (ed.) (1949; reprint 1970).
113   Cf. Day, Mabel, and Robert Steele (eds.) (1936; reprint 1987).

c.1225 (c.1200) ST. MARGARET OF ANTIOCH:[114] Iesu Crist, godes sune, beo þu eauer mi gleo & mi gledunge.

a1300 (c.1150) *The Proverbs of Alfred*:[115] Vre dryhten crist..is one gleaw [vr. gleu] ouer alle glednesse.

The word *glee* collocates with such verbs as *haven* 'make sport', *don a* 'perpetrate a scheme' *maken* 'to rejoice' and *holden* to 'be pleased'. What is more, one can find the word in the following fixed expressions: *me gladieth me no gle* 'I am without pleasure' and *ne gamede hem no gle* 'nothing gave them pleasure'.

However, when we consult the data collected by <u>oed</u>, we learn that another meaning of *glee* that simultaneously developed was 'musical entertainment, playing music, melody'. In order to account for this change, one needs to bear in mind the fact that music played a special role in medieval life, being the most popular form of entertainment of those times, and therefore being one of the possible sources of joy. In the view of Holsinger (2001: 2),

> deep-seated assumptions about musical sonority as a practice of the flesh exerted a clear influence upon the composition, performance, reception, and representation of music from the twelfth throughout the fourteenth century and, further, that music played a central imaginative and ideological role in medieval representations of the human body.

Therefore, music can be compared to the feeling of joy, the latter also being represented in body language. This sense of *glee* vanished from the English language, according to <u>oed</u>, in the 15th century:

Fig. 39. The presence of the lexical item glee *as 'musical entertainment, playing music, melody' in literature according to* <u>oed</u>*.*

```
c1000              c1320
c1000        c1250 a1300 c1440
 ├───┬───┬───┬───┬───┬───┬───┬───┬───┬───┬───┤
 1100 1200 1300 1400 1500 1600 1700 1800 1900 2000 2100
```

The <u>oed</u> quotations below prove the existence of *glee* as 'musical entertainment, playing; music, melody':

c.1000 *The Paris Psalter*: Ealdormenn..gleowe sungon.

a1300 *Cursor Mundi*:[116] Quil wit gleu, and quil wit sang þus he serued saul lang.

c.1440 *Promptorium Parvulorum*: Glu or mynstralcye, *musica, armonia*.

---

114   Cf. Mack, Frances M. (ed.) (1934; reprint 1990).
115   Cf. Arngart, Olaf (ed.) (1955).
116   Cf. Hupe Heinrich (1874–1893).

128

The word soon started to be used with reference to 'an instrument of music' and 'a musical composition'. It appears that not only was music given the status of the major source of joy, but also that of brilliance, another sense developed by *glee* being 'shining brightness'. Thus, *pleien an other glee* is 'to play another instrument'; *maken glee* 'to play music' and *harping glee* 'music on the harp', all collocations given by *med*. Other figurative expressions are mentioned by *oed*, all having to do with music: *glee-book, glee-maiden, glee-singer, glee-singing, glee-beam* 'the harp', as well as *glee-club* 'a society formed for the practice and performance of glees and part-songs'.

In order to account for the domain that serves as the binding tool for all these senses of *glee*, one would seem to be within one's rights to claim that such a domain is that of PLEASURE and ENTERTAINMENT, as visible below:

Fig. 40. The matrix of domains involved in the historical semantics of glee.

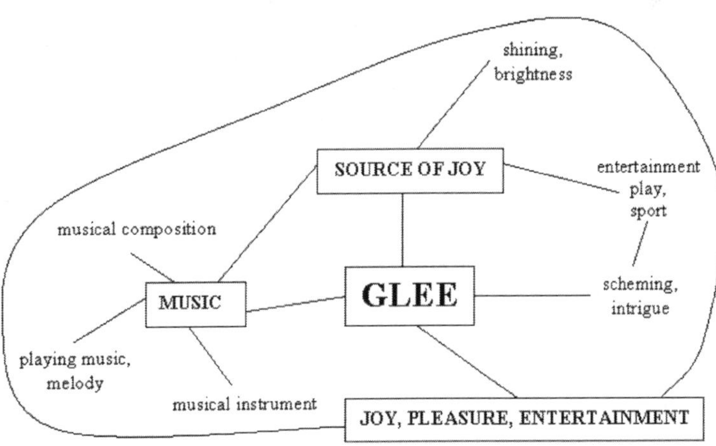

The reason for this is the fact that whatever play or sport one takes into account, it usually serves as a source of entertainment. A very similar approach can be adopted towards scheming and intrigues, and to joy itself. One who feels joyful is willing to taste some entertainment[117] and the reverse. Entertainment is, on many occasions, treated as a source of joy, pleasure.

Furthermore, since the widely accepted form of entertainment in medieval Europe was music, there seems to be no doubt that it started to be treated as glee.

---

117   Out of three verbal collocations of *entertain, LDOCE 5* lists *to enjoy entertainment.*

Last but not least, brightness must have been associated with positive emotions too. It is quite probable that it was also treated as a sort of entertainment.

3.3.8 *Joy*

As the etymological data show, the lexeme *joy* is of French origin, having its roots in OFr *joie, joye* 'joy, jewel'. This, in turn, as noted by <u>oed</u>, corresponds to Latin *gaudia*, the plural of which is *gaudium*, meaning 'joy', but, according to Klein (1966: 833), mistaken for a feminine singular noun. As indicated by <u>oed</u>, the Latin noun has developed from the verbal form *gaudere* 'rejoice', which had been formed from the Proto Indo-European base *gau-*.

The term appeared in the English language in the 13th century and since then it has come a long and complicated way, although usually being referred to as a positive state of mind. On the basis on the data collected by <u>oed</u>, we can conjecture that the factors causing the emotion of pleasure varied, depending, as we can guess, on the values held by the people living in particular periods of time. In other words, the meanings of *joy* appear to have been marked by the mentality of the people who were taught by history that the reasons of joyful emotions can be numerous. Hence, we can observe the development of *joy* from the sense 'a vivid emotion of pleasure arising from a sense of well-being or satisfaction', very often associated with 'exultation of spirit', to 'result, satisfaction, success', the last meaning being given by <u>oed</u> an ironic shade. If one seeks for the possible explanation of such a state of affairs, one is within one's right to refer to the specificity of the times during which these meanings exist. To start with the former sense, we need to state that, as <u>oed</u> points out, the earliest literary quote that proves its existence dates back to 1225:

> a1225 *Ancrene Riwle*:[118] Efter þe spreoue, on ende, beonne is þe muchele ioie.

Examples from later periods include the following:

> 1535 *Biblia*:[119] They that sowe in teeres, shal reape in ioye.

> 1611 The Holy Bible:[120] When the morning starres sang together, and all the sonnes of God shouted for ioy.

It is easy to notice that in most of the quotations the lexical item *joy* is mentioned with reference to religious practices, God or contact with God, in whatever form:

---

118   Cf. Dobson, Eric John (1972)
119   Cf. Coverdale, Miles (transl.) (1535)
120   Cf. *The Holy Bible: 1611 Edition, King James Version* (1982)

130

church service, prayer or a daily song to the glory of the Lord. Therefore, we can say that the very beginnings of this meaning must have had its source in medieval values commonly accepted by both the learned and the peasants. To be precise, God definitely was, and still is, treated as a source of joy,[121] which can be illustrated with the hymn of Bernard of Clairvaux, a medieval French abbot, (_cyberhymnal_):

> Jesus, Thou Joy of loving hearts,
> Thou Fount of life, Thou Light of men,
> From the best bliss that earth imparts,
> We turn unfilled to Thee again.

When it comes to the more recent sense of _joy_, i.e. 'result, satisfaction, success', we need to remember that "[r]eligion and politics – amongst other spheres – no longer shape life and societies as intensively as they used to do, and globalized corporations have an increasing share of shaping lifestyles" (Meinhold 2009: 51) In fact,

> Entering into the mind of the medieval world is very difficult for moderns. There is a vast mental and psychological distance between the twenty-first century and the middle ages. The latter were drenched in mysticism, whereas the contemporary world has been shaped by rationalism so that mystical concepts and experiences have been stripped away except among a small number of people steeped in the religious thought of our Western ancestors. (Harrigan 2002: 113)

As _oed_ shows, _joy_ in the sense 'a vivid emotion of pleasure arising from a sense of well-being or satisfaction; exultation of spirit' existed over seven centuries.

Fig. 41. The notification of the lexical item joy as 'a vivid emotion of pleasure arising from a sense of well-being or satisfaction; exultation of spirit' in literature according to oed.

							1867			
a1240					1651	1785	1820			
a1225	1340	c1440	1535	1611	1754	1802				

1100	1200	1300	1400	1500	1600	1700	1800	1900	2000	2100

Joy 'result, satisfaction, success', often being a negative connotation, had already become popular already in the 20th century:

---

121   Fabiszak (2001: 79) notes that "[n]ow it is not only God, or even the beloved raised to the status of God (lover = _my life's joy_), but anybody who may _do_ or _make somebody joy_.

Fig. 42. The presence of the lexical item joy *as 'result, satisfaction, success' in literature according to* <u>oed</u>*.*

```
                                                    1973
                                                    1972
                                                    1971
                                                    1961
                                                    1961
                                                    1946
                                                    1945
                                                    1945
    ├──────────────────────────────────────────────────────┤
      1100  1200  1300  1400  1500  1600  1700  1800  1900  2000  2100
```

It can also be seen in the following <u>oed</u> quotations:

> 1945 *Tee Emm*:[122] There's even less joy in sending us the money.

> 1973 *Scotsman*:[123] Parking the car in this bay we started to look for a path and a break in the barbed wire-again with no joy.

Other quotes evidencing the aforementioned meaning of *joy* as 'happiness, gladness' are given by <u>med</u>:

> a1450 *York Plays*:[124] Nowe in my sawle grete ioie haue I!

> a1375 *William of Palerne*[125]: So glad was he þanne, þat na gref vnder god gayned to his ioye.

The term *joy* has also carried the meaning of 'merrymaking, revelry', as seen in the following <u>med</u> data:

> c.1350 *Midland Prose Psalter*[126]: Herieþ hym in cymbals of ioie

> a1425 (c.1385) GEOFFREY CHAUCER *Troilus and Criseyde*[127]: What! is this al the joye and al the feste?

Other meanings of *joy*,[128] as found in <u>med</u>, are 'vigour, strength; fervour', 'playfulness', 'pleasure, indulgence; gratification of the senses', as well as 'love, a love affair'

---

122   Cf. *Tee emm* (Air Ministry training magazine, 1941–46 (2015).
123   Cf. Ritchie, John (1817).
124   Cf. Smith, Lucy T. (ed.) (1885).
125   Cf. Bunt, Gerrit H. V. (ed.) (1985).
126   Cf. Bülbring, Karl D. (ed.) (1891; reprint 1987).
127   Cf. Benson, Larry D. (ed.) (1987).
128   It is important to note that the non-religious sense of *joy* is not a recent step in the term's evolution. It has already appeared in Middle English, being as much popular then as it is now. The non-religious sources of *joy* can be different. Fabiszak (2001: 79) mentions several of them: "love, kissing and other bodily pleasures, talking about the

and 'attractiveness, beauty, elegance'. In search of parallels between these senses, one can come up with a common conceptual domain, i.e. that of HAPPINESS/ PLEASURE. It may be assumed that if you achieve success, play, love, feel strong and attractive, you are happy and/or pleased:

Fig. 43. The matrix of domains involved in the historical semantics of joy.

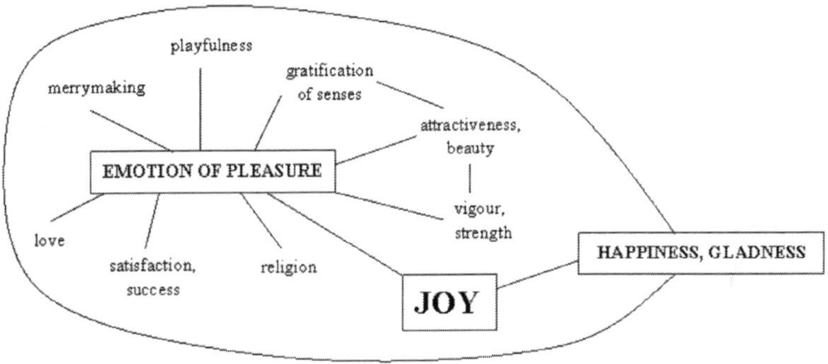

As psychological research shows,

> every emotion must have a cognitive basis and an object (intentionally). There is some corollary debate concerning the status of moods and mood-like emotions (e.g. joy), which do not have a determinate object, but it can be argued that moods do have an object – namely, the world as a whole. "A depressed man lives in a depressed world" wrote Wittgenstein (1953). (Lewis, Haviland-Jones, Barrett 2008: 12)

What might be interesting to note is the fact that the lexeme *joy* has also developed negative senses. Fabiszak (2001: 78), out of 178 occurrences of *joy* in *Confesio Amantis, The Canterbury Tales, The Book of the Duchess, Troilus and Criseyde, Legend of Good Women* and *The Romaunt of the Rose,* has noted several negative connotations. These are: *sorrow* (12),[129] *woe* (8), *pain* (7), *distress* (1), *harm* (1), *hevynesse* 'sorrow' (1), *tribulations* (1), *grief* (1). As she notes, "[i]n most cases the negative feelings are aroused by a disappointment in love, love itself being by far the most common cause of the *earthly joy*" (ibid.), the last issue having been already mentioned.

---

beloved, lover's reunions, meeting or seeing somebody dear, generosity, prosperity, receiving gifts, having a child and another person's misfortune".

129   The numbers in brackets mark the number of occurrences of *joy* in the meanings listed.

As far as more recent connotations of *joy* are concerned, we need to remember that on many occasions the lexeme is compared to *happiness*, these two being sometimes treated as substitutes for each other. In order to analyse the metaphorical expressions of the concept of *joy*, Stefanowitsch (2006: 63–65) accepts Lakoff and Johnson's (1980: 11) distinction between metaphorical concepts (or conceptual metaphors) and metaphorical expressions. While the former are understood as general mental mappings from a source domain (usually concrete) to a target domain (usually abstract), metaphorical expressions are only instances of these mappings, in the form of individual linguistic items. Thus, "[w]hat constitutes [a] metaphor is not any particular word or expression. It is the ontological mapping across conceptual domains" (Lakoff 1993: 208).

Therefore, dealing with the domain (BASIC) EMOTIONS, Stefanowitsch (2006: 66) comes up with the notion of a metaphorical pattern analysis (henceforth MPA), where a metaphorical pattern is seen as "a multi-word expression from a given source domain (SD) into which one or more specific lexical item from a given target domain (TD) have been inserted". It would appear that finding a proper term representing the domain of pleasure, satisfaction, comfort and bliss is not an easy task. Both *happiness* and *joy* seem to be appropriate. However, it turns out that it is the word *joy* that seems the better choice for this function. This is due to the fact that, as she notes, the word appears in the British National Corpus almost one-and-a-half times more frequently than *happiness*. Furthermore, the word *joy* tends to be more frequently employed in metaphorical expressions. These, as studied by Stefanowitsch (2006: 83–84), are presented in Table 3:

Table 3. Metaphorical patterns manifesting HAPPINESS metaphors posited in the literature, as analysed by Stefanowitsch (2006: 83–84).

HAPPINESS/BEING HAPPY IS	NUMBER OF OCCURRENCES IN LITERATURE
UP	2
X be elated with joy, joy be lifted	
BEING OFF THE GROUND	12
X('s heart) jump/leap for/with joy	
BEING IN HEAVEN	0
-	

HAPPINESS/BEING HAPPY IS	NUMBER OF OCCURRENCES IN LITERATURE
LIGHT *sunny joy, glow/radiance of joy, X's face light up/shine with joy, joy shine in/lighten X's face, X's eyes be bright/luminous with joy, X light Y's eye with joy, X radiate joy, X beams with joy, X reflect joy, joy dim, X blot out joy*	18
VITALITY/HEALTH *X's eyes be alive with joy*	1
WARM *melting joy, joy generates warmth, X blush with joy, warm joy*	4
AN ANIMAL THAT LIVES WELL *-*	0
A PLEASURABLE PHYSICAL SENSATION *-*	0
FLUID IN A CONTAINER *heart swell with joy, X swell heart with joy, joy pour into heart, X brim over with joy, joy seep from X, overflowing joy*	6
CAPTIVE ANIMAL *X unleash joy, joy be unconfined/unrestrained*	4
OPPONENT IN A STRUGGLE *overwhelming joy, X be/feel overcome with joy, X beat/defeat/kill joy*	7
A RAPTURE/HIGH *heady joy, ecstasy of joy*	3
INSANITY *delirious joy*	1
A NATURAL FORCE *Flood/surge of joy, joy surges through X, joy sweeps over/through X, X be swept away by joy, joy subside*	7
HEAT/FIRE *seething joy, flare/sparks of joy, joy be spark, X smother joy, X burn with joy*	6
A LIQUID *effervescent joy, source/spring of joy, flow/river of joy, joy spring from X, X drink joy*	11
A SUBSTANCE IN A CONTAINER (UNDER PRESSURE) *inner joy, X be filled with/full of joy, X contain joy, X fill Y('s) heart with joy, X leave Y empty of joy, X's heart fill with joy, explosion of joy, X explode/burst with joy, joy burst in X's heart, joy burst through X, X erupt in joy*	38

HAPPINESS/BEING HAPPY IS	NUMBER OF OCCURRENCES IN LITERATURE
A MIXED/PURE SUBSTANCE *pure/unalloyed joy, mixed joy, mixture of emotion and joy, emotion combine with joy, X combine emotion with joy*	19
A DESTROYABLE OBJECT *X break/destroy/mar Y's joy*	7
DISEASE *sick joy, joy be infectious, joy befall X, X feel sick with joy, X die of joy*	5
AGGRESSIVE ANIMAL BEHAVIOUR *fierce/wild/savage joy*	6
AN ORGANISM *growing/short-lived joy, fruit of joy*	7
TOTAL	164

It is easy to see that, taking the first case of metaphors as an example, *X be elated with joy* or *joy be lifted* are only instances, i.e. metaphorical expressions, of the conceptual metaphor HAPPINESS IS UP. However, contrasting mappings for *happiness*[130] and *joy*, Stefanowitsch (2006: 96–97) comes to the conclusion that the mapping for *happiness* is TRYING TO ATTAIN AN EMOTION IS SEARCHING FOR AN EMOTION, whereas *joy* is characteristic of two mappings: BEING/ACTING IN AN EMOTIONAL STATE IS BEING ACCOMPANIED BY AN EMOTION and BEING HAPPY IS BEING UP/OFF THE GROUND. Thus, it seems easy to notice that

> [t]he motivation for this difference can presumably be found in our (culturally mediated) perception of the role that the two emotions play in our lives: while *happiness* and *joy* refer to similar emotions, HAPPINESS is potentially a less intensely experienced emotional state (…), and hence potentially a more stable one and one whose attainment is more easily conceptualized as being the responsibility of the experiencer. Thus, it is

---

130 Stefanowitsch (2006: 97) mentions the following mappings for *happiness*, instantiated by the following metaphorical patterns:
   a) TRYING TO ATTAIN HAPPINESS IS SEARCHING: *pursuit of happiness, route/ path/way to happiness, X be in search of happiness, snatch at happiness, stretch out hand for happiness*;
   b) ATTAINING HAPPINESS IS FINDING SOMETHING: *happiness seem within reach, X attain happiness, X find happiness, X reach happiness*;
   c) NOT BEING ABLE TO ATTAIN HAPPINESS IS INABILITY TO REACH SOMETHING: *X stand in way of happiness, happiness elude X, happiness be irretrievable.*

possible to actively look for HAPPINESS (and hold on to it once it is found), while the more intense, short-lived JOY can only be stumbled upon by chance (…) (ibid., p.98)

A very similar viewpoint on the matter is taken by Tissari (2008: 170–171), for whom *happiness* is a kind of norm, whereas *joy* has connotations with something that is beyond the ordinary, the latter usually resulting in behavioural reactions and physiological effects.

3.3.9 *Mirth*

The word *mirth* is, according to <u>oed</u>, a cognate with Middle Dutch *marchte, merechte* 'joy, pleasure', these having much in common with the adjective *merry*. It appeared in the English language in the Early Old English period, as evidenced by <u>oed</u>:

Fig. 44. The presence of the lexical item mirth *as 'joy, pleasure' in literature according to* <u>oed</u>.

```
OE                        a1586
OE          c1230 a1393 c1451   1554   1696
eOE c1175 a1225 c1300 c1400 a1500   1659
  ├─────────────────────────────────────────────┤
   1100  1200  1300  1400  1500  1600  1700  1800  1900  2000  2100
```

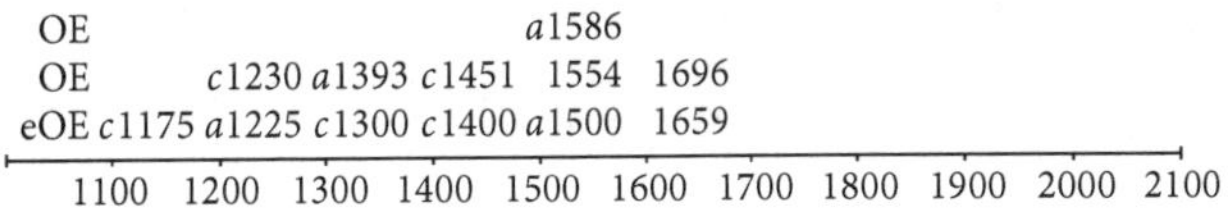

and denoted 'pleasurable feeling; enjoyment; gratification; joy; happiness', often having religious connotations. The sense is documented in the following <u>oed</u> quotations:

c.1230 (a1200) *Ancrene Riwle:*[131] Treowe ancres beoð a riht briddes of heouene..ant ase beo þe sigeð habbeð murhðe of heorte.

1696 N. TATE & N. BRADY *New Version Psalms* ii. 11 Rejoyce with awful Mirth.

The plural form of *mirth* soon started to be associated with 'delights, joys', thus again being given the sense of positive feelings and emotions that accompany a happy person throughout his/her lifetime. As suggested by the literary quotes, the word *mirth* was occasionally given the meaning of 'a cause of joy'. Although, as the etymological data point out, this usage of *mirth* is an obsolete one:

Fig. 45. The presence of the lexical item mirth *as 'a cause of joy' in literature according to* <u>oed</u>.

```
OE          c1225        a1450
  ├─────────────────────────────────────────────┤
   1100  1200  1300  1400  1500  1600  1700  1800  1900  2000  2100
```

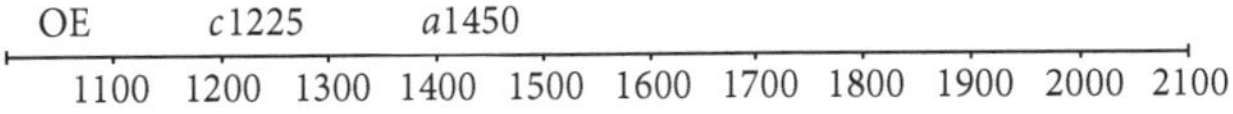

131   Cf. Dobson, Eric John (1972).

It is within one's rights to claim that this sense is not an accidental semantic stage in the evolution of the term. After all, it has been a rather common occurrence that, as evidenced in the analysis of other words meaning 'joy', a term primarily designating 'joy, happiness' sooner or later starts bearing the sense of 'a cause of joy'. As *oed* shows, there have been only three occurrences of mirth as 'a cause of joy':

> OE *Rune Poem*: byþ mære metodes leoht, myrgþ and tohiht eadgum and earmum.

> c.1225 (c.1200) *St. Katherine*: þe is mi lauerd & mi luue, mi lif & mi leofmon, mi wunne.. mi murhðe & mi mede.

> a1450 *York Plays*: Itt was full mekill myrþe to þe þat I schulde ligge in wombe of þine.

As for the possible sources of *mirth*, Fabiszak (2001: 80) mentions listening to music, sexual intercourse, the beauty of nature, interaction with other people and entertainment. The data collected by *med* also suggest that *mirth* can be triggered by a marvellous phenomenon, a felicitous event, as can be seen in:

> c.1175 *Homilies in Bodley*:[132] Þa for3eat he..alle þas eorðlic þing..& wace heo him þuðten for þa murhþe þe he þa iseah.

> a1300 *Maximian*:[133] Is wille he heuede I-nou, And pal wor prude he drou And oþere murþes mo.

> c.1540 (a1400) *Destruction of Troy*:[134] With qwistlis & qwes & other qwaint gere, Melody of mowthe, myrthe for to here.

as well as beauty or attractiveness, which is shown in:

> c1175 *Homilies in Bodley*:[135] Þe deofel hæfde middaneardes murhþe & all weorldlice fe3ernesse togædere æthiwod.

> a1398 JOHN TREVISA *Bartholomaeus's De Proprietatibus Rerum*:[136] Þe sonne is þe y3e of þe worlde, myrþe of þe day, feyrnesse of heuen.

> a1500 *Prose Legend of the Cross Before Christ*:[137] He..bihield the amenite, melodie, and myrth that no tung of man may shewe ne tel.

---

132   Cf. Belfour, A. O. (ed.) (1909; reprint 1988).
133   Cf. Brown, Carleton (ed.) (1932).
134   Cf. Panton, George A. and David Donaldson (eds.) (1869, 1874; reprint as one vol. 1968)
135   Cf. Belfour, A. O. (ed.) (1909; reprint 1988).
136   Cf. Seymour, Michael C. and Gabriel M. Liegey, and others (eds.) (1975).
137   Cf. Hill, Betty (1965).

138

Since *mirth* is also 'an entertainment or amusement', it can be expressed through the singing of birds and musical performance, as is clearly seen in these quotations:

> c.1275 (a1200) LAYAMON *The Brut*:[138] Bemen þer bleowen..þer weore segge songe, þer were pipen þer wes swa muchel murehðe þat ne mihte heo beon na mare.

> a1375 WILLIAM OF PALERNE:[139] So wel hit him liked, þe sauor of þe swete sesoun & song of þe briddes þat [it]..layked him long while to lesten þat merþe.

Furthermore, a reason for *mirth* can also be the telling of jokes and stories. This is evidenced by the following <u>med</u> quotations:

> c.1390 GEOFFREY CHAUCER, *Canterbury Tales: Physician-Pardoner Link, Pardoner's Prologue, Tale, and Epilogue*[140]: Tel vs som myrthe or iapes.

> c.1460 (c.1400) *Beryn*:[141] When all this..feleship were com..with talys glad & merry, Som of sotill centence, of vertu & of lore, And som of othir myrthis, for hem þat hold no store Of wisdom, ne of holynes, ne of Chiualry.

The lexeme *mirth* has entered a lot of collocations during its long semantic evolution process. The data collected by <u>med</u> list a number of such collocations. Thus, we can *drauen mirth* 'obtain happiness', *geten mirth* 'be happy', *haven mirth* 'rejoice', *maken mirth* 'be delighted, happy', *meten mirth* 'achieve happiness', *missen mirth* 'be deprived of happiness', *taken mirth* 'be delighted'. We can *comen to mirth* 'be amused, entertained', *connen of it* 'be a raconteur', *don, tellen mirth* 'entertain, amuse', *maken mirth* 'entertain'. The lexical item also enters such collocations as *don wonder and mirthe* 'to do miraculous deeds', *ben mirthe* 'be a blessing', *mirthe in hering* 'delightful to hear', *melen materes of* 'to broach a pleasant subject', *nevnen mirthe* 'exchange pleasantries', *spel of mirthe* 'entertaining story', *pleies and mirthe* 'theatrical performances'.

It should be mentioned that, in the course of its semantic evolution, not only did *mirth* develop the sense 'a cause of joy', but it also acquired the meaning 'the expression or manifestation of joy or happiness', often bearing a different character. Hence, as <u>med</u> notes, *mirth* can be expressed through a ceremony, festivity, recreation, which can be seen in the following quotations:

> c.1395 GEOFFREY CHAUCER *Canterbury Tales: Clerk's Prologue and Tale*:[142] Euery man and womman dooth his myght This day in murthe and reuel to dispende.

---

138 Cf. Brook, George L. and Robert F. Leslie (eds.) (1963, 1978).
139 Cf. Bunt, Gerrit H. V. (ed.) (1985).
140 Cf. Manly, John M. and Edith Rickert (eds.) (1940).
141 Cf. Furnivall, Frederick J. and Walter G. Stone (eds.) (1909; reprint 1973).
142 Cf. Manly, John M. and Edith Rickert (eds.) (1940).

a1500 (a1415) JOHN MIRK, *Festial*:[143] Þys ys a pryncypall salue..to put away all maner worldes vanyte and vayn murthe and reuell.

It appears that the aforementioned 'sexual dalliance,[144] love-making' is not only a form of manifestation of *mirth*, but also one of the term's meanings. This is testified by the following quotes:

c.1390 GEOFFREY CHAUCER *Canterbury Tales: Shipman's Tale*:[145] Al that nyght in myrthe they bisette.

c.1500 (?c1450) *The Wedding of Sir Gawain and Dame Ragnell*:[146] He made myrthe alle in her boure And thankyd of alle oure Sauyoure.

Hence, *maken mirthe* acquired a new sense. Not only did it mean 'to celebrate, to have fun', but it was also found in the context of 'to make love, have intercourse'. Of the possible ways of expressing *mirth*, Fabiszak (2001: 81) also lists laughter and kissing. The term *mirth* is strongly related to the word *joy*, which is evident not only in the semantic data, but also in psychological research:

Identifying the behavioural and physiological characteristics of different positive emotions is made challenging by inconsistent terminology in the current literature. For example, humorous stimuli (e.g. comedy film clips) have been used to elicit emotional states described as "joy" (…), "mirth" (…), "amusement" (…), "happiness" (…), and even "exhilaration" (…). In addition, positive emotion terms such as "joy" and "mirth" have been used somewhat interchangeably (…), and combined descriptors such "happiness / amusement" (…) and "joy / laughter" (…) are often used (Herring, Burleson, Roberts, Devine, 2011: 211).

If we correctly deduce from the quotation, *joy* and *mirth* have always been tightly interwoven with one another as well as with other *joy* lexemes, both on the semantic and psychological level. After all, psychology as the study of the relationship between human behaviour and the mind is deeply rooted in semantics which deals with the study of the meanings of words.

It has been mentioned on many occasions that many words denoting *joy* have usually been associated with religion, and thus used in the sense 'religious joy, heavenly bliss'. *Mirth* is no exception. In the data collected by *med* one can find the term under consideration as 'eternal bliss, salvation, the joys of heaven':[147]

---

143 Cf. Erbe, Theodor (ed.) (1905; reprint 1987).
144 The sexual connotations of *mirth* are also evidenced by Shipley (1955: 87) who, defining the term *baudery*, a variant of bawdry, describes it as 'gaiety, mirth'.
145 Cf. Manly, John M. and Edith Rickert (eds.) (1940).
146 Cf. Sumner, Laura (ed.) (1924).
147 Bloomfield (2009: 2), associating mirth with God, joy, laughter and happiness, defines the term as "gladness accompanied with laughter".

c.1175 *Homilies in Bodley*:[148] Eadi3e beoð þa ðeowæs..for þam þe he heom set ofer alle his gode, þæt is, ofer alle neorcxnæwonges murhðe.

a1500 *Sidrak and Bokkus*:[149] Þe good to heuene þe weie shullen take Where ioye and merþe shal neuere slake.

However, *mirth* is also popular as 'salvation, eternal life', as well as 'God, Christ', the latter sense evidenced by the quotations below:

c.1400 (c.1380) *Cleanness*:[150] For traysoun..Man may mysse þe myrþe þat much is to prayse..And in þe Creatores cort com never more.

c.1475 *Earth Upon Earth*:[151] In heywyn to dweylle..That myrthe for to myse it wer a karful case..That myrth is withowttyn ende.

As far as fixed expressions of a religious character are concerned, these are *meine of mirthe* 'saints in heaven', *bringen to mirthen* 'to restore to eternal life', *comen/ gon/wenden to mirthe* 'be saved', *meten with mirthe* 'attain salvation', *ben met with mirthe* 'be blessed', *meten mirthen* 'grant the joy of salvation' and *forlesen/lesen/ missen mirthe* 'forfeit salvation'.

In search of parallels between all of the aforementioned senses of *mirth* one has good grounds to state that the domain binding them all is the domain of HAPPINESS/GLADNESS, as visible in the matrix of domains if the lexeme:

Fig. 46. The matrix of domains involved in the historical semantics of mirth.

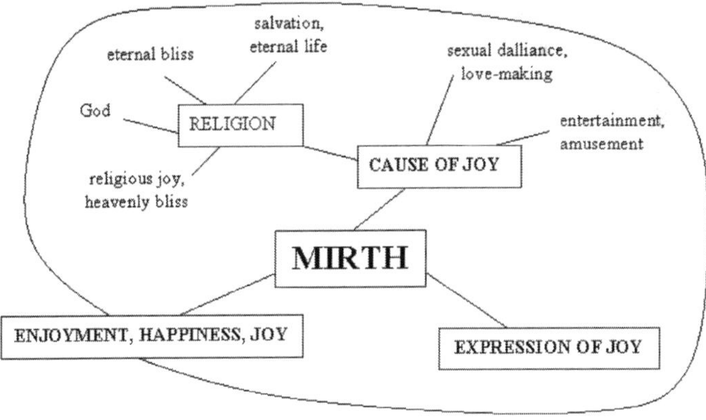

148   Cf. Belfour, A. O. (ed.) (1909; reprint 1988).
149   Cf. Burton, Tom L. (ed.) (1998).
150   Cf. Menner, R. J. (ed.) (1920).
151   Cf. Murray, Hilda M. R. (ed.) (1911; reprint 1964).

The reason for such a choice of the tool grouping all of these senses is the fact that the sense of pleasure, enjoyment and joy is incorporated into the definition of MIRTH. It can be stated that the cause of positive emotions in whatever dimension is at the same time a cause of happiness and gladness. Hence, all the sources of *mirth* must, at the same time, trigger gladness and feelings of happiness. After all, music, singing, beauty, love, feast, jokes, etc. can be classified as factors that positively influence the mind, contributing to the rise of a feeling of gladness and happiness. Furthermore, it seems natural that the overall feeling of gladness leads to its overt manifestation. Last but not least, God and salvation have always been treated, in the eyes of the faithful, as a source of happiness.

3.4 The evolution of the English 'joy' vocabulary: the results

The study of English 'joy' vocabulary, as conducted in the present book, was based on the theory of language by Ronald Langacker (1987, 1988, 1990, 1991, 1994, 1998, 1999, 2002, 2008, 2009, 2011a, 2011b, 2015), especially the issue of language conceptualisation and that of cognitive domains as a way of grouping vocabulary together. Moreover, because the study had a historical character, Przemysław Łozowski's (1993, 1999, 2000, 2005, 2008, 2010, 2011, 2012a, 2012b, 2012c, 2014) understanding of panchrony as language change plus cognition was treated as the key parameter for the analysis of the semantic change of the lexical items denoting 'joy'. It seems that the semantic paths of the analysed lexical items have been different, yet have a common conceptual domain which can be perceived as the semantic tool that binds their senses together, forming the domain of JOY. To be more specific, the lexical items that became the subject matter of historical semantic research in this book are these that have survived till the present times and have developed the meaning of 'joy' in their semantic evolution. As has been shown, the semantics of *bliss, cheer, delight, dream, game, gladness, glee, joy* and *mirth* points to their common underlying conceptual domain JOY. Such a conclusion can be seen in Table 4:

Table. 4. Conceptual domains binding the senses of 'joy' terms.

LEXEME	MEANINGS	COGNITIVE DOMAIN BINDING THE MEANINGS
bliss	– 'spiritual exultation or ecstasy' – 'heavenly bliss, the joys of heaven' – 'heaven, paradise' – 'the splendour or majesty of God, divine glory' – 'good fortune, prosperity, well-being' – 'rejoicing, merrymaking, festivity' – 'a source of joy, a cause of happiness; sexual gratification' – 'joy, happiness, pleasure'	domain of HAPPINESS/ PLEASURE
cheer	– 'face' – 'the face or presence of God' – 'the face as expressing emotion, attitude or character, mien' – 'a gesture or act indicative of an attitude or intention' – 'behaviour, manner, or an instance of it' – 'good cheer or humour; gladness, happiness, joy'	domain of GLADNESS/ EMOTION
delight	– 'an emotion of pleasure, esp. sensuous delight; sexual gratification' – 'pleasure, joy' – 'charm, delightfulness; the quality which causes delight'	domain of PLEASURE
dream	– 'joy, pleasure, gladness, mirth' – 'the sound of a musical instrument, especially a bell, trumpet etc.' – 'voice, speaking' – 'singing, a song'	domain of GLADNESS
game	– 'joy, happiness, delight, gaiety, mirth, amusement' – 'festivity, revelry, amusement, play, music' – 'love-making' – 'a joke or jest' – 'any of the sports of hunting, fishing, hawking or fowling' – 'the animal hunted' – 'wild animals' – to 'an athletic contest, sport in which people compete with each other'	domain of PLEASURE

LEXEME	MEANINGS	COGNITIVE DOMAIN BINDING THE MEANINGS
gladness	– 'joy, cheerfulness' – 'a pleasurable condition, state of happiness' – 'alacrity, cheerful readiness' – 'kindness, gentleness, favourable consideration, favour' – 'delight, pleasure' – 'brightness'	domain of HAPPINESS/ CHEERFULNESS
glee	– 'entertainment, play, sport' – 'scheming, intrigue' – 'mirth, joy, bliss, pleasure, delight' – 'a source of joy' – 'musical entertainment, playing music, melody' – 'an instrument of music' – 'a musical composition' – 'shining brightness'	domain of PLEASURE/ ENTERTAINMENT
joy	– 'a vivid emotion of pleasure arising from a sense of well-being or satisfaction' – 'exultation of spirit' – 'result, satisfaction, success' – 'happiness, gladness' – 'merrymaking, revelry' – 'vigour, strength; fervour' – 'playfulness' – 'attractiveness, beauty, elegance'	domain of HAPPINESS/ PLEASURE
mirth	– 'pleasurable feeling; enjoyment; gratification; joy; happiness' – 'delights, joys' – 'a cause of joy' – 'an entertainment or amusement' – 'the expression or manifestation of joy or happiness' – 'a sexual dalliance, love-making' – 'eternal bliss, salvation, the joys of heaven' – 'salvation, eternal life'	domain of HAPPINESS / GLADNESS

Concentrating on the words analysed, it seems right to state that 'joy' words tend to be associated with a variety of sources. The relationship between the sources of joy and the words denoting 'joy' are presented in Table 5.

Table 5. Sources of joyful emotions vs. 'joy' lexemes.

TYPE	NO.	SOURCE	'JOY' WORD
I	1.	religious experience	*bliss, cheer, dream, game, gladness, joy, mirth*
	2.	martyrdom	*gladness*
II	3.	having a child	*bliss, gladness, joy*
III	4.	socialising	*game, mirth*
IV	5.	well-being/prosperity/success	*bliss, joy*
V	6.	festivity	*bliss, cheer, delight, game, joy, mirth*
	7.	dancing	*Cheer*
	8.	music, singing	*delight, dream, game, gladness, glee, mirth*
	9.	entertainment, e.g. sport	*Delight, game, glee, mirth*
	10.	the beauty of nature, walking	*gladness, mirth*
	11.	hunting, chasing sports	*game, gladness*
	12.	jokes, laughter, telling stories	*game, mirth*
VI	13.	bodily pleasure	*bliss, delight, game, joy, mirth*
VII	14.	a beloved person	*bliss, joy*
	15.	meeting/seeing somebody dear	*gladness, joy*
	16.	love	*gladness, joy*
	17.	lovers' reunion	*cheer, gladness*
VIII	18.	generosity	*Joy*
	19.	receiving gifts	*Joy*
IX	20.	another person's failure	*gladness, glee, joy*
X	21.	beauty, attractiveness	*joy, mirth*

In order to briefly analyse the results shown in Table 5, one needs to take into consideration the fact that, similar to Fabiszak's (2001: 85) research, we can divide these sources of joyful emotions which are profiled within the appropriate categories into several types:

I. Religious experience: *bliss, cheer, dream, game, gladness, joy, mirth* (7);
II. Family life: *bliss, gladness, joy* (3);
III. Socialising: *game, mirth* (2);
IV. Possession/success: *bliss, joy* (2);

V.   Entertainment: *bliss, cheer, dream, delight, game, gladness, glee, joy, mirth* (9);
VI.   Bodily pleasure: *bliss, delight, game, joy, mirth* (5);
VII.   Romantic love: *bliss, cheer, joy, gladness* (4);
VIII.   Deeds of positive value: *joy* (1);
IX.   Deeds of negative value: *gladness, glee, joy* (3);
X.   Beauty: *joy, mirth* (2).

The numbers in brackets signify the number of 'joy' words as caused by given factors. One can deduce that the most popular reason for joyful emotions has been entertainment of some sort. It is worthy noting, at the turn of the 21st century, and in the era of constant rush, that government programmes have appeared encouraging people to engage in a variety of pastimes. In the words of Cushman, Veal and Zuzanek (2005: 2), authorities

> at national, regional and local levels, throughout the world, are heavily involved in supporting and promoting such sectors of leisure as: sport, physical recreation, and education; outdoor recreation in urban and natural areas; children's play; the arts; natural and cultural heritage; and broadcasting.

This could explain why all of the nine 'joy' terms analysed signify their sources in entertainment of different forms. Thus, one has good grounds to state that *bliss, cheer, delight, dream, game, gladness, glee, joy* and *mirth* have all evolved into the sense of 'joy of entertainment'.

Another popular source of joy is to be found in religious experience of any kind. This can be God's presence, contact with the Lord, spiritual exultation, glory, heaven and even martyrdom. As it turns out from the analysis carried out in this book, seven lexical items denoting 'joy' have followed their paths of semantic evolution in such a direction that, sooner or later, they started to denote 'joy of religion'. The reason for such historical semantics of *bliss, cheer, dream, game, gladness, joy* and *mirth* can be found in the fact that religious experience has always been an essential part of human life. After all, God says: "[t]hese things I have spoken to you, that My joy may remain in you, and that your joy may be full" (John 15: 11, *NT*). For this very reason,

> [j]oy is a delight in life that runs deeper than pain or pleasure. This type of joy stems from an awareness of God's presence in one's life, allowing us to rise above circumstances and focus on the goodness and love of God. At the core of Christian joy is the fact that God has acted and is acting to save those who trust in Him (Goldstein 2010: 22).

The analysis of the evolution of English 'joy' vocabulary shows that another quite popular source of joy has been found in bodily pleasures. The big likelihood of finding joy in kisses, hugs and love-making must have contributed to the development of the sense 'joy of body' in five lexical items: *bliss, delight, game, joy* and *mirth*. However, "while Epicurus states that bodily pleasure is the original seat of spiritual joy, he too, recognizes that sensual pleasure is not at all the true goal of life" (Kittel and Friedrich 1985: 304).

What appears to bring little joy are, surprisingly, deeds of positive value. Only one term 'joy' is associated with this sort of pleasure. There turn out to be other seemingly joyful elements of life, but not joyful enough to make many lexical items develop their meanings of 'joy'. To be precise, only two words, i.e. *game* and *mirth,* have semantically evolved to mean 'joy of socializing'. Furthermore, while only *bliss* and *joy* have developed the sense 'joy of possession/success', two words, this time *joy* and *mirth,* have again become associated with 'joy of beauty'.

Therefore, on the basis of the analysis carried out in the present book, the evolution of English 'joy' vocabulary is, to a great extent, shaped by the culture of the people living in different periods of time, e.g. by their life values and doctrines. Thus, we reflect our lifestyles, habits, cultures, etc., in the language we use, especially the semantics of vocabulary. This is because "language does not exist apart from culture, that is, from the socially inherited assemblage of practices and beliefs that determines the texture of our lives" (Sapir 1921: 170–171).

It is worth noting that, as careful scrutiny has shown, not all the lexical items, although all present in today's English, have retained the sense 'joy'. Although both *dream* and *game* somehow have taken their semantic paths in different directions, their "joyful" senses are still to be found in their collocations. Thus, if something works *like a dream*, it works 'extremely well or effectively', thus, probably, causing joy. Something or someone can *be a dream*, i.e. 'perfect or desirable', hence they can be a source of joy. When it comes to the word *game*, it exists in the fixed expression *make game of somebody*, which means 'make fun of somebody'. This collocation can, as we already know, be treated as a deed of negative value, and thus a potential source of joy.

3.5 Conclusion

In search of the motivating mechanisms behind semantic developments of the English 'joy' vocabulary, we have elaborated on the vision of language and cognition, and cognitive domains according to Langacker (1987, 1988, 1990, 1991, 1994, 1998, 1999, 2002, 2008, 2009, 2011a, 2011b, 2015), as well as the theory of panchrony (language change plus cognition) according to Łozowski (1993, 1999, 2000, 2005, 2008, 2010, 2011, 2012a, 2012b, 2012c, 2014).

The objective of Chapter 3 was to show the panchrony of English lexical items denoting 'joy'. For this reason, joy as an emotion was shown, together with its linguistic and psychological aspects. The paths of the semantic evolution of *bliss, cheer, delight, dream, game, gladness, glee, joy* and *mirth* have been analysed, and particular attention has been paid to the sources of these kinds of joy. Through reference to cognitive domains, proposed as the constructs that bind all the senses of the words under consideration, we can conclude that it is the sources of joy that have pushed these 'joyful' lexical items in the directions of their semantic evolution, as presented in Chapter 3, and hence serve as the motivating parameters behind these sense alterations. It is interesting to note that out of the nine analysed 'joy' terms present in Modern English seven appear to have survived to the present day in the sense 'joy'. The social and psychological sources of these positive emotions have contributed to meaning changes of the lexical items concerned. To sum up, there are good grounds to state that the most popular sources of joy are that of entertainment, religion and the body.

Conclusions

In this book we have assumed that words are related in a variety of ways. Sense relations have been presented both from the structural and the cognitive point of view, cognitive linguistics being treated as a functional alternative to field theory. The major reason why the apparatus of semantic fields has been replaced with cognitive linguistics is the fact that the notion of the semantic field does not exceed relations between lexical items. Such a state of affairs is difficult to accept, for it is not words themselves that set their relations with other words but the determinant of sense relations is to be sought in the human mind, hence in thought. To account for these phenomena we need to take note of perception, reasoning and categorisation, taking into account the extralinguistic factors that influence language. These are cultural habits, experience, cognition, impressions, etc. What is more, the linking of sense relations has been presented on two levels, conceptual domains being given the status of the linguistic tool that binds meanings. Hence, not only does a domain bring together different senses of one word, but it also binds senses of different words. To be more precise, the background for this book was the theory of language and cognition and cognitive domains according to Ronald Langacker (1987, 1988, 1990, 1991, 1994, 1998, 1999, 2002, 2008, 2009, 2011a, 2011b, 2015), as well as the theory of panchrony (language change plus cognition) according to Przemysław Łozowski (1993, 1999, 2000, 2005, 2008, 2010, 2011, 2012a, 2012b, 2012c, 2014). First, in the opinion of Langacker (2008: 43–44), the notion of meaning cannot be dealt with without the notion of *construal*, which is understood as the ability to conceive and portray the same situation in alternative ways. Moreover, according to Langacker (2008: 44), an expression or a word invokes a cognitive domain or a set of cognitive domains, where a cognitive domain is understood as any kind of conception or realm of experience. To be more specific, it is our experience that influences thought, and thought that shapes language. If what people think about the world changes, then language changes as well. This, consequently leads us to the theory of panchrony as proposed by Łozowski, where panchrony is viewed as language change plus cognition. This is how language change is explained by the cognitive factors of human existence.

The study of English 'joy' vocabulary has been performed within the spirit of cognitive linguistics and panchrony, as described above. It concentrates on those lexical items that, having appeared in Old, Middle or Modern English, denote 'joy' or, having referred to 'joy' in the past, have retained their 'joy' sense in collocations until these times. The analysis of the historical semantics of *bliss, cheer, delight, dream, game, gladness, glee, joy* and *mirth* shows not only the linguistic features of the terms concerned, but can also serve as a linguistic picture of social life in the Anglo-Saxon countries. In other words, the identification of the sources of joy gives an idea of what life looked like throughout the centuries and how people's preferences of spending their lifetime changed. The different stimuli for joyful emotions can serve as a wide panorama of various life philosophies popular in different epochs, starting in the Middle Ages and continuing until the recent times.

Medieval life, as one can suppose from the analysis of the historical semantics of the 'joy' vocabulary, concentrated on the pure spiritual life, joy being derived from God, prayer, the presence of the Lord, glory, spiritual exultation, heaven, relief from suffering, eternal life or even martyrdom. The beginning of the Renaissance and the revival of the ancient *carpe diem* postulate made people aware that there were far more other aspects of life to enjoy and seize. Life, instead of being God-oriented, became human- and human body-oriented, as evidenced in the historical semantic paths of the 'joy' words. Joy of the senses and body is clearly observable in the potential sources of all nine 'joy' words analysed in this book. The semantics of *bliss, cheer, dream, delight, game, gladness, glee, joy* and *mirth* points to such stimuli of pleasures as those that result in entertainment and bodily delight. While the former is usually caused by festivity, eating, drinking, dancing, singing, nice voice, beautiful views, laughter and playing sport, the latter tends to be achieved through kissing, hugging and love-making.

Hence, on the basis of this research, one can assume that it is the stimuli for joy that appear to be the motivating mechanisms behind the semantic developments of the English 'joy' vocabulary. This is visible in the natural tendency of the lexemes under discussion to semantically evolve in such directions that their senses reflect different sources of joyful emotions associated with the words through the centuries. Thus, one has good ground to assume that it is religious experience, so popular in medieval life, that pushed OE *bliss* 'joy, kindness of manner' (*oed*) to specialise its meaning in the spiritual context. Hence, *bliss* is 'spiritual exultation or ecstasy', 'the joys of heaven', 'heaven', 'the splendour of God'. The bond between medieval life and the term *bliss* which had already appeared in the English language already in the 10th century is thus explained by the popular sources of joy at the time when the word appeared and evolved.

In search of more examples of lexemes the semantics of which has been shaped by the popular sources of 'joy' in given periods of time, one may refer to a term that entered the English lexicon at the turn of the Middle Ages and the Renaissance. What is important to note is the fact that in the 13th century, when the lexical item *delight* appeared in the English language, a new way of thinking was

150

being initiated, presupposing that cognition comes through sensory experience, and this can be treated as the motivation parameter influencing the semantic evolution of the term mentioned above. *Delight*, the primary meaning of which is 'pleasure, joy', evolved semantically to become associated with 'sexual gratification'. Hence, on the basis of the analysis carried out in the present book, one may have good grounds to state that sensory pleasure was such a popular source of joy that it triggered the sense specialisation of the lexeme *delight*.

However many sources of joy are to be sought in life shaped by the philosophy of its times, one needs to remember that the stimulus for this positive emotion does not necessarily lie in philosophy itself. Any source of joy, whether influenced by social and philosophical ideas or not, can function as the motivating mechanism behind the semantic developments of the English 'joy' vocabulary. For example, the lexeme *joy* itself has specialised to mean 'a vivid emotion of pleasure arising from a sense of well-being or satisfaction', 'exultation of spirit', 'satisfaction, success', 'merrymaking, revelry', 'vigour, strength' and 'playfulness'. Hence, one can assume that the sources of joy associated with this word have been wealth, success, religious experience, festivity, humour and strength.

We can assume, from the research carried out in Chapter 3, that whatever sources of joy there are, there is a hierarchy of the popularity of joy stimuli. It appears that the sphere of life which is most likely to be considered to be a cause for joy is entertainment – all nine terms have developed in the direction of the sense 'joy of entertainment'. The semantic evolution of seven words to the sense 'joy of religion' suggests that the second popular source of the positive emotion in question is religious experience. The third common stimulus for joy is, as can be seen from the study, corporeal pleasure associated with kisses, hugs and love-making. This is evident in the semantic evolution of five lexemes which developed the sense 'joy of body'.

Looking at the concept of joy from the linguistic perspective, the motivating factor behind organising different senses of a word is a conceptual domain. One can assume that all senses of a word have a common feature, which makes it possible for them to be specified by one conceptual domain. For example, the senses of *glee* cover 'entertainment, play, sport', 'scheming, intrigue', 'mirth, joy, bliss, pleasure, delight', 'a source of joy', 'musical entertainment, playing music, melody', 'an instrument of music', 'a musical composition', 'shining brightness'. It can be supposed that the conceptual domain that joins them all is the domain of PLEASURE and ENTERTAINMENT. After all, they all can and do serve as sources of joyful emotions. When one takes into account the word *mirth*, one may speculate that the domain under which all its meanings can be grouped is the domain of HAPPINESS/

GLADNESS. The meanings 'pleasurable feeling; enjoyment; gratification; joy; happiness', 'delights, joys', 'a cause of joy', 'an entertainment or amusement', 'the expression or manifestation of joy or happiness', 'a sexual dalliance, love-making', 'eternal bliss, salvation, the joys of heaven', 'salvation, eternal life' suggest that the different sources of joy, i.e. entertainment, amusement, love-making, eternal bliss, or salvation, evoke a feeling of happiness and gladness.

However, what needs to be remembered is that conceptual domains operate not only on the level of the meanings of a word, bringing them together. In fact, conceptual domains also work on a higher level, binding senses of different words. Therefore, if one supposes that the domain that binds the senses of *cheer* is GLADNESS/EMOTION, the domain characteristic of the senses of *bliss* is HAPPINESS/PLEASURE, the domain involved in the historical semantics of *mirth* is HAPPINESS/GLADNESS, the domain building the senses of *gladness* is HAPPINESS/CHEERFULNESS, the domain common for senses of *dream* is GLADNESS, the domain bringing together the senses of *delight* and *game* is PLEASURE, whereas *glee* is characterised by PLEASURE/ENTERTAINMENT and *joy* by HAPPINESS/PLEASURE, then one may assume that the one common conceptual domain for all these words is the domain of JOY. The justification for this conclusion is to be sought in the definition of the lexeme *joy*: *LDOCE 5* defines it as 'great happiness and pleasure', and *dictionary* as 'the emotion of great delight or happiness caused by something exceptionally good or satisfying; keen pleasure; elation'. What is more, according to *m-w*, *joy* is 'the emotion evoked by well-being, success, or good fortune or by the prospect of possessing what one desires'. All the definitions can be calibrated into a coherent picture. Joy is an emotion of happiness, gladness or pleasure, caused by something satisfying, e.g. entertainment. Hence, conceptual domains do indeed serve as the motivating force behind bringing meanings together. Not only do domains join senses of one word, but they also work at a higher level, linking the senses of different words.

References

AITCHISON, JEAN (1995) *Language Change: Progress or Decay?*, Cambridge: Cambridge University Press.

ALLAN, KEITH (2001) *Natural Language Semantics*, Oxford: Blackwell.

ANONYMOUS (1522) *Here begynneth a propre newe interlude of the worlde and the chylde* (1522) 1st edition, 1 vol., London: Wynkun de Worde.

ARNGART, OLAF (ed.) (1955) *The Proverbs of Alfred*, Lund: Gleerup.

ARNGART OLAF (ed.) (1968) *The Middle English Genesis and Exodus*, pp. 54–158, Lund: Gleerup.

APRESJAN, JURIJ (1966) "Analyses distributionnelles des significations", in: *Langages* 1. pp. 44–74.

BABCOCK GOVE, P. (1995) *Webster's Third New International Dictionary of the English Language*, Cologne: Könemann.

BAILLIE-GROHMAN, WILLIAM A. AND FLORENCE BAILLIE-GROHMAN (eds.) (1904) *The Master of Game by Edward, Second Duke of York*, London: Ballantyne, Hanson.

BALLY, CHARLES (1940) "L'Arbitraire du signe", in: *FM*, vol. 8. pp. 193–206.

BARBOUR, JOHN (1375) *The Bruce*, Aberdeen: The Spalding Club (published 1856, retrieved 2008).

BAUMGÄRTNER KLAUS (1967) "Die Struktur des Bedeutungsfeldes", in: H. Moser (ed.), *Satz und Wort im heutigen Deutsch*, pp. 165–197, Düsseldorf: Schwann.

BAWCUTT, PRISCILLA (ed.) (1998) *The Poems of William Dunbar*, 2 vols, Glasgow: Association for Scottish Literary Studies.

BENSON, LARRY D. (ed.) (1987) *The Riverside Chaucer*, 3rd ed., pp. 473–585, Boston: Houghton Mifflin.

BELFOUR, A. O. (ed.) (1909; reprint 1988) *Twelfth Century Homilies in MS Bodley 343*, London: Oxford University Press.

BENSON, LARRY D. (ed.) (1987) *The Riverside Chaucer*, 3rd ed., Boston, Massachusetts: Houghton Mifflin Company.

BERGEN, HENRY (ed.) (1906, 1906, 1910; reprint as one vol. 1996) *Lydgate's Troy Book*, parts 1–3, London: Kegan Paul, Trench, Trübner and Co.

BERLIN, BRENT AND PAUL KAY (1969) *Basic Color Terms: Their Universality and Evolution*, Berkeley: University of California Press.

BLOCK, KATHERINE S. (ed.) (1922; reprint 1961) *Ludus Coventriae or the Plaie Called Corpus Christi*, London: Oxford University Press.

Bloomfield, Edward (2009) "The Worth of Mirth", First Congregational Church, California: Long Beach, http://www.firstchurchlb.org/Sermon/090222_Sermon.pdf

Bramley, Henry R. (ed.) (1884) The Psalter and Certain Canticles in English by Richard Rolle of Hampole, Oxford: Clarendon Press.

Bright, William (1992) *International Encyclopedia of Linguistics Volume 1*, 1st edition, Oxford: Oxford University Press.

Brinton, Laurel J. and Elizabeth Closs Traugott (2005) *Lexicalization and Language Change*, Cambridge: Cambridge University Press.

Brook, George L. and Robert F. Leslie (eds.) (1963, 1978) *Laȝamon's Brut*, Oxford: Oxford University Press.

Brook, George L. (1968) *Harley Lyrics*, Manchester: Manchester University Press.

Brown, Carleton (ed.) (1932) *English Lyrics of the XIIIth Century*, pp. 15–16, Oxford: Clarendon Press.

Brown, Colin M. and Peter Hagoort (1999) "The cognitive neuroscience of language", in: Brown Colin M. and Peter Hagoort (eds.) *The Neurocognition of Language*, pp. 5–14.

Bruno, Giordano (1591) *De Imaginum, signorum & Idearum compositione, Ad omnia Inventionum, Dispositionum & Memoriae genera Libri tres*, Francofurti, (translation 1991: *On the Composition of Images, Signs and Ideas*, Dick Higgins (ed.), New York: Willis, Locker & Owens).

Bülbring, Karl D. (ed.) (1891; reprint 1987) *The Earliest Complete English Prose Psalter*, New York: Kraus Reprint.

btasd = *the Bosworth-Toller Anglo-Saxon Dictionary*, http://bosworth.ff.cuni.cz/

Bunt, Gerrit H. V. (ed.) (1985) *William of Palerne: An Alliterative Romance*, Groningen: Bouma's Boekhuis.

Burkhanov, Igor (1999) "Field theory: The state of the art and its implications for ideography", in: *Zeszyty Naukowe Wyższej Szkoły Pedagogicznej w Rzeszowie*, Zeszyt 32/1999, pp. 51–73.

Burton, Tom L. (ed.) (1998) *Sidrak and Bokkus*, vol. 1., Oxford: Oxford University Press.

Butler, Chris S. and Miriam Taverniers (2008) "Layering in Structural-Functional Grammar", in: Johan van der Auwera (ed.), *The Interdisciplinary Journal of the Language Sciences–Linguistics*, pp. 690–695, Berlin: Mouton de Gruyter.

Buttler, Danuta (1967) "Koncepcje pola znaczeniowego", in: *Przegląd Humanistyczny*, 2, pp. 41–59.

CASSON, LESLIE F. (ed.) (1949; reprint 1970) *The Romance of Sir Degrevant*, even pp. 2–114, London: Oxford University Press.

CHEN, PEILEI (2010) "A Cognitive Study of "Happiness" Metaphors in English and Chinese Idioms", in: *Asian Culture and History*, vol. 2, pp. 172–175, Toronto: Canadian Center of Science and Education.

CHRYSOSTOM, JOHN *(1986) Homilies on Genesis, (trans.) Robert C. Hill, Washington, D.C.: Catholic University of America Press.*

CLAUSNER, TIMOTHY C. AND WILLIAM CROFT (1999) "Domains and image schemas", in: *Cognitive Linguistics* 10-1, pp. 1–31.

COSERIU, EUGENIO (1967) "Lexikalische Solidaritäten", in: *Poetica*, vol. 1, pp. 293–303.

COSERIU, EUGENIO AND HORST GECKELER (1981) *Trends in Structural Semantics*, Narr: GunterNarr Verlag Tübingen.

COVERDALE, MILES (transl.) (1535) *Biblia: The Bible, that Is, the Holy Scripture of the Olde and New Testament, Faithfully and Truly Translated Out of Douche and Latyn Into Englishe*, Southwark: J. Nycolson.

CROFT, WILLIAM (1993) "The role of domains in the interpretation of metaphors and metonymies", in: *Cognitive Linguistics* 4-4, pp. 335–370.

CROFT WILLIAM (2006) "Evolutionary models and functional-typological theories of language change", in: Ans van Kemenade and Bettelou Los (eds.) *The Handbook of the History of English*, Oxford: Blackwell Publishing Ltd.

CRUSE, DAVID ALAN (1975) "Hyponymy and lexical hierarchies", in: *Archivum Linguisticum* 6, pp. 26–31.

CRUSE, DAVID ALAN (2011) *Meaning in Language: An Introduction to Semantics and Pragmatics*, 3rd edition, Oxford: Oxford University Press.

CUSHMAN, GRANT, A.J. VEAL, AND JIRI ZUZANEK (2005) "Leisure Participation and Time-use Surveys: an Overview", in: Grant Cushman, A.J. Veal, and Jiri Zuzanek (eds.) *Free Time and Leisure Participation: International Perspectives*, pp. 1–16, Oxfordshire, Cambridge: CABI Publishing.

cyberhymnal = http://www.cyberhymnal.org/htm/j/t/jthoujoy.htm

DAY, MABEL AND ROBERT STEELE (eds.) (1936; reprint 1987) *Mum and the Sothsegger*, pp. 1–26, London: Early English Text Society/Oxford University Press.

DEVRIES, F. C. (ed.) (1966) *Floris and Blauncheflur, a Middle English Romance*, Gröningen: Drukkerij V.R.B.

dictionary = http://dictionary.reference.com

DIRVEN, RENÉ AND MARJOLIN VERSPOOR (2004) *Cognitive Exploration of Language and Linguistics*, 2nd revised edition, Amsterdam and Philadelphia: John Benjamins Publishing Company.

Dobson, Eric John (1972) *The English text of the Ancrene Riwle*, London: Oxford University Press.

Dongen, van G.A. (1933) *Amelioratives in English*, Rotterdam: T. De Vries, Dz.

Dornseiff, Franz (1938) "Das Problem des Bedeutungswandels", in *Zeitschrift für deutsche Philologie* 63, pp.119–138.

Durkin, Philip (2009) *The Oxford Guide to Etymology*, New York: Oxford University Press.

Earle, John (ed.) (1865) *Saxon Chronicles,* Oxford: Clarendon Press.

Ehrensperger, E. C. (1931) "Dream Words in Old and Middle English", in: *PMLA* 46, pp. 80–89.

Erbe, Theodor (ed.) (1905; reprint 1987) *Mirk's Festial: A Collection of Homilies by Johannes Mirkus (John Mirk)*, London: Early English Text Society/Oxford University Press.

Evans, Vyvyan and Melanie Green (2006) *Cognitive Linguistics: An Introduction*, Edinburgh: Edinburgh University Press.

Fabiszak, Małgorzata (2000) "An application of the Natural Semantic Metalanguage to diachronic semantics", in: Irma Taavitsainen, Terttu Nevalainen, Päivi Pahta, and Matti issanen (eds.), *Placing Middle English in Context*, pp. 293–312, Berlin: Mouton de Gruyter.

Fabiszak, Małgorzata (2001) *The concept of 'joy' in Old and Middle English: A semantic analysis*, Piła: Wyższa Szkoła Biznesu.

Fauconnier, Gilles (1988) "Quantification, Roles and Domains", in: Umberto Eco, Marco Santambrogio, and Patrizia Violi (eds.) *Meaning and Mental Representations*, pp. 61–80, Bloomington: Indiana University Press.

Fauconnier, Gilles (1997) *Mappings in Thought and Language*, Cambridge: Cambridge University Press.

Fauconnier, Gilles and Mark Turner (2002) *The Way We Think. Conceptual Blending and the Mind's Hidden Complexities*, New York: Basic Books.

Fischer, Rudolf (1903, 1904) "Vindicta Salvatoris", in: *Archiv* 111, 112 vol. 11, pp. 289–98; vol. 12, pp. 25–45.

Forshall, John and Frederic Madden (eds.) (1850) *The Holy Bible by John Wycliffe and His Followers*, Oxford: Oxford University Press.

Fowler, Joseph Thomas (ed.) (1891) *The life of Saint Cuthbert in English Verse*, Surtees Society 87, Durham: Andrews and Co.

French Walter Hoyt and Charles Brockway Hale (eds.) (1930) *Middle English Metrical Romances*, pp. 383–419, New York: Prentice-Hall.

Friederici, Angela D. (2002) "Towards a neural basis of auditory sentence processing", in: *TRENDS in Cognitive Sciences* 6 (2), pp. 78–84.

Furnivall, Frederick J. (ed.) (1866; re-ed. 1903; reprint 1965) *Political, Religious, and Love Poems,* pp. 80–111, London: Early English Text Society/Oxford University Press.

Furnivall, Frederick J. and Walter G. Stone (eds.) (1909; reprint 1973) *The Tale of Beryn with a Prologue of a Merry Adventure of the Pardoner with a Tapster at Canterbury,* London: Early English Text Society/Oxford University Press.

GDSQ (2008) = *Gaither's Dictionary of Scientific Quotations,* Carl C. Gaither and Alma E. Cavazos-Gaither, p. 1231, New York: Springer.

Geeraerts, Dirk (2010) *Theories of Lexical Semantics,* New York: Oxford University Press.

George, Teresa (2006) *How to be Happy: A Practical Guide,* Twickenham: Athena Press.

Gerbier, Balthazar (1662) A brief discourse concerning the three chief principles of magnificent building, London.

Ginzburg, R.S., S.S. Khidekel, G.Y. Knyazeva, and A.A. Sankin (1966) *A Course in Modern English Lexicology,* Moscow: Higher School Publishing House.

glp = *Germanic Lexicon Project,* http://web.ff.cuni.cz/cgi-bin/uaa_slovnik/gmc_search_v3?cmd=formquery2&query=&startrow=1

Głaz, Adam, David S. Danaher, and Przemysław Łozowski (eds.) (2013) *The Linguistic Worldview. Ethnolinguistics, Cognition, and Culture,* London: Versita.

Goldstein, Clifford R. (ed.) (2010) "The Fruit of the Spirit is Joy", in: *The Fruit of the Spirit,* http://www.absg.adventist.org/2010/1Q/SE/PDFs/EAQ110_03.pdf

Gordon, Terrence W. (1982) *A History of Semantics,* Amsterdam/Philadelphia: John Benjamins Publishing Company.

Gower, John (1390) (R. Pauli 1857; English Works, E.E.T.S. 1900) *Confessio amantis.*

Grattan, John H. G. and G. F. H. Sykes (eds.) (1935; reprint 1973) *The Owl and the Nightingale,* London: Early English Text Society/Oxford University Press.

Greene, Henry Graham (1938) *Brighton Rock: a novel,* 1st edition, 1 vol., New York: Heinemann.

Greet, William C. (ed.) (1927; reprint 1987) *The Reuele of Crysten Religioun,* pp. 1–509, London: Early English Text Society/Oxford University Press.

Griffiths, Bill (ed.) (1994) *Alfred's Metres of Boethius,* Rev. ed. Pinner, UK: Anglo-Saxon Books.

GRYGIEL, MARCIN (2012) *In Search of a Cognitive Linguistic Model of Semantic Change*, Saarbrücken: Lambert Academic Publishing.

GUIRAUD, PIERRE (1976) *Semantyka*, Warszawa: Wiedza Powszechna (originally published as *La Sémantique* (1971), trans. Stanisław Cichowicz).

HALL, JOSEPH (ed.) (1920) *Selections from Early Middle English*, 2 vols., pp. 176–96, London: Oxford University Press.

HARRIGAN, ANTHONY (2002) "The Medieval Mind: A Meditation", in: *Humanitas*, vol. XV, No. 2, pp. 113–119.

HEINE, BERND, ULRIKE CLAUDI, AND FRIEDERIKE HUNNEMEYER (1991) *Grammaticalization: A conceptual framework*, Chicago: University of Chicago Press.

HERRING, DAVID R., MARY H. BURLESON, NICOLE A. ROBERTS, AND MICHAEL J. DEVINE (2011) "Coherent with laughter: Subjective experience, behavior, and physiological responses during amusement and joy", in: *International Journal of Psychophysiology* 79, pp. 211–218.

HILL, BETTY (1965) "The Fifteenth-Century Prose Legend of the Cross before Christ", in: *Medium Ævum* 34, pp. 203–222.

HOLSINGER, BRUCE W. (2001) *Music, Body, and Desire in Medieval Culture*, Stanford: Stanford University Press.

HORSTMANN, CARL (ed.) (1887; reprint 1987) The Early South-English Legendary from Bodleian MS. Laud Misc. 108, London: Trübner and Co.

HORSTMANN, CARL (ed.) (1892; reprint 1987) *The Minor Poems of the Vernon MS*, part 1, 106–20, London: Kegan Paul.

HUMBOLDT, WILHELM VON (1836) Über die Verschiedenheit des menschlichen Sprachbaues und ihren Einfluß auf die geistige Entwickelung des Menschengeschlechts, Hg. von Eduard Buschmann, Berlin: Dümmler.

HUPE, HEINRICH (1874–1893) "Cursor Mundi. The Cursur of the World. A Northumbrian poem of the XIVth century, in four versions", in: Morris, Richard (ed.), London: Kegan Paul, Trench, Trübner and Co.

HUSSEY, RICHARD CHARLES (1947) *Historical Geology: The Geologic History of North America*, New York: McGraw-Hill Book Company.

IPSEN, GUNTHER (1924) "Der alte Orient und die Indogermanen", in: Friedrich, J. (ed.), *Stand und Aufgaben der Sprachwissenschaft. Festschrift für Streitberg*, pp. 200–237. Heidelberg: Winter.

JOLLES, ANDRÉ (1934) "Antike Bedeutungsfelder", in: *PBB*, *lviii*, pp. 97–109.

KAMBOJ, JIYA LAL (1986) *Semantic Change in Sanskrit*, Delhi: Vinod Kumar Sharma Nirman Prakashan.

KARDELA, HENRYK (2007) "*Good* revisted: A mental spaces analysis", in: Ulf Magnusson, and Henryk Kardela (eds.), *Further Insights into Semantics and Lexicography*, Lublin: Wydawnictwo Uniwersytetu Marii Curie-Skłodowskiej.

KEYSER, CASSIUS JACKSON (1927) *Mole Philosophy and Other Essays*, New York: E. P. Duffon & Company.

KITTEL, GERHARD AND GERHARD FRIEDRICH (eds.) (1985) *Theological Dictionary of the New Testament*, Michigan: William B. Eerdmans Publishing Company.

KIVISTÖ, SARI (2008) "Sour Faces, Happy Lives? On Laughter, Joy and Happiness of the Agelasts", in: Heli Tissari, Anne Birgitta Pessi and Mikko Salmela (eds.), *Happiness: Cognition, Experience, Language. Collegium Studies across Disciplines in the Humanities and Social Sciences* 3, pp. 79–100, Helsinki: Helsinki Collegium for Advanced Studies.

KLEIN, ERNEST (1966) *A Comprehensive Etymological Dictionary of the English Language*, Vol. 1, Amsterdam, London, New York: Elsevier Publishing Company.

KLEPARSKI, GRZEGORZ A. (1983) "Lexical mobility; some problems of its justification and interpretation", in: *Kwartalnik Neofilologiczny*, vol. 30, pp. 3–12.

KLEPARSKI, GRZEGORZ A. (1997) Theory and Practice of Historical Semantics: The Case of Middle English Synonyms of GIRL/YOUNG WOMAN, Lublin: Redakcja Wydawnictw Katolickiego Uniwersytetu Lubelskiego.

KLEPARSKI, GRZEGORZ A. AND ANGELINA RUSINEK (2007a) "Field Theory and Diachronic Semantics", in: Grzegorz A. Kleparski, Robert Kiełtyka, and Marta Pikor-Niedziałek (eds.), *Aspects of Semantic Transposition of Words*, pp. 75–88, Chełm: Wydawnictwo TAWA.

KLEPARSKI, GRZEGORZ A. AND ANGELINA RUSINEK (2007b) "The Tradition of Field Theory and the Study of Lexical Semantic Change", *Studia Anglica Resoviensia* 4.

KLEPARSKI, GRZEGORZ A. AND ANGELINA RUSINEK (2008) "On the Conceptual Contiguity of the Conceptual Categories CLOTHES and HUMAN BEING", in: Grzegorz A. Kleparski, and Agnieszka Uberman, (eds.), *Galicia Studies in Language, Literature and Culture with Special reference to English and Diachronic Semantics*, pp. 41–49, Chełm: Wydawnictwo TAWA.

KOCK, ERNST A. (ed.) (1902; reprint 1987) Three Middle-English Versions of the Rule of St. Benet., EETS 120.

KOWALEWSKI, HUBERT (2016) Motivating the Symbolic. Towards a Cognitive Theory of the Linguistic Sign, Frankfurt am Main: Peter Lang.

Labov, William (1973) "The boundaries of words and their meaning", in: Charles-James N. Bailey and Roger W. Shuy (eds.), *New ways of analyzing variation in English*, pp. 340–373, Washington D.C.: Gorgetown University Press.

Lakoff, George (1993) "The contemporary theory of metaphor", in: Andrew Ortony (ed.) *Metaphor and Thought*, 2nd edition, pp. 202–251, Cambridge, Cambridge University Press.

Lakoff, George and Mark Johnson (1980), *Metaphors We Live By*, Chicago: University of Chicago Press.

Langacker, Ronald W. (1987) *Foundations of Cognitive Grammar*, Vol. 1, Stanford, California: Stanford University Press.

Langacker, Ronald W. (1988) "A Usage-Based Model", in: Rudzka-Ostyn, Brygida (ed.) *Topics in Cognitive Linguistics. Current Issues in Linguistics Theory 50*, pp. 127–161, Amsterdam and Philadelphia: John Benjamins.

Langacker, Ronald W. (1990) "Cognitive Grammar: The Symbolic Alternative", in: *Studies in the Linguistic Sciences 20*, pp. 3–30.

Langacker, Ronald W. (1991) *Foundations of Cognitive Grammar*, vol. 2, Stanford, California: Stanford University Press.

Langacker, Ronald W. (1994) "Culture, Cognition, and Grammar", in: Martin Pütz (ed.), *Language Contact and Language Conflict*, pp. 25–53, Amsterdam and Philadelphia: John Benjamins.

Langacker, Ronald W. (1998) *Conceptualization, Symbolization, and Grammar*, Tomasello, Michael (ed.), *The New Psychology of Language: Cognitive and Functional Approaches to Language Structure*, pp. 1–39, Mahwah, NJ and London: Erlbaum.

Langacker, Ronald W. (1999) *Grammar and Conceptualization*, Berlin & New York: Mouton de Gruyter.

Langacker, Ronald W. (2002) *Concept, Image, and Symbol. The Cognitive Basis of Grammar*, 2nd edition, Berlin and New York: Mouton de Gruyter.

Langacker, Ronald W. (2008) *Cognitive Grammar: A Basic Introduction*, New York: Oxford University Press.

Langacker, Ronald W. (2009) *Investigations in Cognitive Grammar*, Berlin and New York: Mouton de Gruyter.

Langacker, Ronald W. (2011a) "Culture, Cognition, and Lexical Meaning", in: Turewicz, Kamila (ed.), *Cognitive Methodologies for Culture-Language Interface: From Lexical Category to Stereotype through Lady Macbeth Speech*, pp. 11–36, Łódź: Wydawnictwo Akademii Humanistyczno-Ekonomicznej.

Langacker, Ronald W. (2011b) "Conceptual Semantics, Symbolic Grammar, and the *day after day* Construction", in: Sutcliffe, Patricia, William J. Sullivan,

160

and Arle Lommel (eds.), *LACUS Forum 36: Mechanisms of Linguistic Behavior*, pp. 3–24, Houston: LACUS.

LANGACKER, RONALD W. (2015) "Construal", in: Dąbrowska, Ewa and Dagmar Divjak (eds.), *Handbook of Cognitive Linguistics*, pp. 120–143, Berlin and Boston: De Gruyter Mouton.

LAYAMON (1963–1978) *Brut: Layamon*, Oxford: Oxford University Press.

LDCE (1978) = *Longman Dictionary of Contemporary English*, Della Summers (ed.), Longman Education Limited (3rd edition).

LDOCE 5 (2009) = Longman Dictionary of Contemporary English, 5th edition, London: Longman.

LEECH, GEOFFREY N. (1981) *Semantics*, Hardsworth: Penguin.

LEHRER, ADRIENNE (1974) *Semantic Fields and Lexical Structure,* Amsterdam & London: North – Holland.

LEHRER, ADRIENNE (1977) "Structures of the lexicon and transfer of meaning", in: *Lingua* 45: pp. 95–123.

LEWIN, KURT (1936) *Principles of Topological Psychology*, New York: McGraw-Hill.

LEWIS, MICHAEL, JEANNETTE M. HAVILAND-JONES AND LISA BARRET (eds.) (2008) *Handbook of emotions*, New York: The Guilford Press.

LIEB, HANS (1978) "On the notion of lexical field", in: *Linguistic Associations of Canada and the United States LACUS-FORUM*, vol. 5, pp. 66–80.

LLULL, RAMÓN (1645/1970) *Ars generalis ultima*, Mallorca. Repr. Frankfurt: Minevra.

LIPKA, LEONHARD (1980) "Methodology and representation in the study of lexical fields", in: Dieter Kastovsky (ed.), *Perspektiven der lexikalischen Semantik. Beiträge zum Wuppertaler Semantikkolloquium vom 2.-3. Dezember 1977*, Bonn: Bouvier Verlag Herbert Grundmann.

LIPKA, LEONHARD (1990) An Outline of English Lexicology. Lexical Structure, Word Semantics, and Word-Formation, Tübingen: Max Niemeyer Verlag.

LYONS, JOHN (1977) *Semantics,* vol. 1, Cambridge: Cambridge University Press.

ŁĄKOWSKI, RAFAŁ (ed.) (1983) *Encyklopedia Powszechna PWN,* vol. 1, Warszawa: Państwowe Wydawnictwo Naukowe.

ŁOZOWSKI, PRZEMYSŁAW (1993) "The Metaphorical Development of the English *dream*. In Search for the Missing Link", in: Elżbieta Górska (ed.), *Images from the Cognitive Scene*, pp. 115–123, Kraków: Universitatis.

ŁOZOWSKI, PRZEMYSŁAW (1999) "Panchrony, or Linguistics without Synchrony", in: Lewandowska-Tomaszczyk, Barbara (ed.), *Cognitive Perspectives on Language*, pp. 23–36, Frankfurt am Mein: Peter Lang.

Łozowski, Przemysław (2000) *Vagueness in Language: from Truth-Conditional Synonymy to un-Conditional Polysemy*, Lublin: Wydawnictwo Uniwersytetu Marii Curie-Skłodowskiej.

Łozowski, Przemysław (2005) "Polysemy in context: *meten* and *dremen* in Chaucer", in: Ritt, Nikolaus and Herbert Schendl (eds.), *Rethinking Middle English: Linguistic and Literary Approaches, (Studies in English Medieval Language and Literature 10.)*, pp. 125–146, Frankfurt am Main: Peter Lang.

Łozowski, Przemysław (2008) *Language as Symbol of Experience: King Alfred's cunnan, magan and motan in a Panchronic Perspective*, Lublin: Wydawnictwo UMCS.

Łozowski, Przemysław (2010) "Językoznawstwo na przełomie wieków: od systemu do symbolu", in: Karwatowska, Małgorzata and Adam Siwiec (eds.), *Przeobrażenia w języku i komunikacji medialnej na przełomie XX i XXI wieku*, pp. 89–99, Chełm: Państwowa Wyższa Szkoła Zawodowa w Chełmie, Chełmskie Towarzystwo Naukowe.

Łozowski Przemysław (2011) "Tradycja jako panchronia, czyli w poszukiwaniu ciągłości kultury", in: Adamowski, Jan and Marta Wójcicka (eds.), *Tradycja w kontekstach kulturowych, (Tradycja dla współczesności. Ciągłość i zmiana 4.)*, pp. 113–123, Lublin: Wydawnictwo UMCS.

Łozowski Przemysław (2012a) "The word as a symbol of experience: from 'satisfied' to 'unhappy' in sad?", in: Przemysław Łozowski and Anna Włodarczyk-Stachurska (eds.), *Words in contexts: from linguistic forms to literary functions*, Radom: Wydawnictwo Politechniki Radomskiej.

Łozowski Przemysław (2012b) "Experience behind language: panchronic motivation behind Polish names of the months", in: *Eugeniusz Cyran, Henryk Kardela, Bogdan Szymanek (eds.)* Sound Structure and Sense. Studies in Memory of Edmund Gussmann, *Lublin: Wydawnictwo KUL*.

Łozowski Przemysław (2012c) "*W poszukiwaniu terminologii językoznawczej: system w czasach symbolu czy symbol na potrzeby systemu?*", in: *Dorota Brzozowska and Władysław Chłopicki (eds.)* Termin w językoznawstwie, Kraków: Tertium.

Łozowski Przemysław (2014) "Od semantyki do gramatyki, czyli o wyższości panchronii nad synchronią i diachronią", in: Małgorzata Gębka-Wolak, Joanna Kamper-Warejko, Andrzej Moroz (eds.), *Leksyka języków słowiańskich w badaniach synchronicznych i diachronicznych*, pp. 89–100, Toruń: Wydawnictwo Naukowe Uniwersytetu Mikołaja Kopernika.

Macaulay, George C. (ed.) (1900; reprint 1978) *The English Works of John Gower*, 2 vols., London: E.E.T.S. E.S. 81, 82.

162

MACK, FRANCES M. (ed.) (1934; reprint 1990) *Seinte Marherete, from MS. Bodley 34 and British Museum MS. Royal 17 A.xxvii*, London: Oxford University Press.

MAGOUN, FRANCIS PEABODY JR. (ed.) (1929) *The Gests of King Alexander of Macedon*, pp. 121–170, Cambridge: Harvard University Press.

MALDONADO, RICARDO (2004) "Ronald Langacker: A visit to Cognitive Grammar", in: *Annual Review of Cognitive Linguistics* 2, pp. 305–319, Amsterdam and Philadelphia: John Benjamins Publishing Company.

MANLY, JOHN M. AND EDITH RICKERT (eds.) (1940) *The Text of the Canterbury Tales*, Chicago: University of Chicago.

MATHER, FRANK JEWETT JR. (1897) *King Ponthus and the Fair Sidone*, Modern Language Association.

MATORÉ, GEORGES (1951) *Le Vocabulaire et la société sous Louis-Philippe*, Geneva: Lille.

MATORÉ, GEORGES (1953) *La Méthode en lexicologie*, Paris : Dider.

McKNIGHT, G.H. (1925) *English Words and Their Background*, New York-London: McGrath Publishing Company.

<u>med</u> = *Middle English Dictionary,http://quod.lib.umich.edu/m/med/med_ent_search.html*

MEILLET, ANTOINE (1921) *Linguistique historique et linguistique generale*, Paris: É. Champion.

MEINHOLD, ROMAN (2009) "Popular Culture and Consumerism: Mediocre, (Schein-) Heilig and Pseudo-Therapeutic", in: Imtiyaz Yusuf and Canan Atilgan (eds.), *Religion, Politics and Globalization. Implications for Thailand and Asia*, pp. 51–65, Bangkok: Konrad Adenauer Stiftung.

MENNER, R. J. (ed.) (1920) *Purity*, YSE 61.

MERREL D. CLUBB, JR. (ed.) (1953) *The Middle English Pilgrimage of the Soul*, University Michigan dissertation.

MEYER, RICHARD MORITZ (1910) "Bedeutungssysteme", in: *Zeitschrift für vergleichende Sprachforschung* 43, pp. 352–368.

MILLER, ROBERT L. (1968) *The Linguistic Reality Principle and Humboldtian Ethnolinguistics*, The Hague: Mouton.

MOFFAT, DOUGLAS (ed.) (1987) *The Worcester Fragments*, pp. 62–81, East Lansing: Colleagues Press.

MORRIS, RICHARD (1872; reprint 1988) *An Old English Miscellany*, pp. 141–44, London: Early English Text Society/Oxford University Press.

MORRIS, RICHARD. (ed.) (1873; reprint 1973) *Old English Homilies*, ser. 2, Oxford: The Clarendon Press.

MORRIS, RICHARD (ed.) (1874; reprint 1961) *Cursor Mundi,* London: Oxford University Press.

MÜLLER, E. (1865) "Ein pessimistischer Zug in der Entwicklung der Wortbedeutungen", in: *Zur Englischen Etymologie - Program Coethen,* pp. 23–35.

MURPHY, LYNNE M. (2003) *Semantic Relations and the Lexicon: Antonymy, Synonymy, and Other Paradigms,* Cambridge: Cambridge University Press.

MURRAY, HILDA M. R. (ed.) (1911; reprint 1964) *The Middle English Poem Erthe Upon Erthe,* pp. 24–26, Early English Society.

m-w = *Merriam Webster* http://www.merriam-webster.com/dictionary

NERLICH, BRIGITTE AND DAVID D. CLARKE (1992) "Outline of a model for semantic change", in: Günter Kellermann and Michael D. Morrissey, *Diachrony within Synchrony: Language History and Cognition. Papers from the International Symposium at the University of Duisburg, 26–28 March 1990,* pp. 125–141, Frankfurt-am-Main: Peter Lang.

NT = (1966) *Nowy Testament. New Testament,* New York: American Bible Society.

OATLEY, KEITH (2004) *Emotions: A Brief History,* Oxford: Blackwell Publishing.

odo = *Oxford Dictionaries,* http://oxforddictionaries.com/

oed = *Oxford English Dictionary,* http://dictionary.oed.com

OED (1971) = *The Oxford English Dictionary,* James Murray, Henry Bradley, Charles Talbut Onions, and William Craigie, Oxford: Oxford University Press.

ÖHMAN, SUSANNE (1951) *Wortinhalt und Weltbild. Vergleichende und methodologische Studien zu Bedeutungslehre und Wortfeldtheorie,* Stockholm: Norstedt & Söner.

ÖHMAN, SUSANNE (1953) "Theories of the Linguistic Field", *Word* 9, pp. 123–134.

OKSAAR, ELS (1958) *Semantische Studien im Sinnbereich der Schnelligheit,* Stockholm: Almqvist & Wiksell.

online ed = *Online Etymology Dictionary,* http://www.etymonline.com/index.php?search=&searchmode=none

PAIN, FREDERIC (2014) Towards a panchronic perspective on a diachronic issue: the rhyme in Old Burmese, in: *HAL.*

PANTON, GEORGE A. AND DAVID DONALDSON (eds.) (1869, 1874; reprint as one vol. 1968) *The Gest Hystoriale of the Destruction of Troy,* London: John Childs and Son, reprinted: Oxford: Oxford University Press.

PAUL, H. (1880) *Prinzipien der Sprachgeschichte,* Tubingen: Max Niemeyer Verlag.

PEIRCE, CHARLES SANDERS (1992) *The Essential Peirce: Selected Philosophical Writings (1867–1893),* Nathan Hauser, and Christian J. W. Kloesel (eds.), Bloomington and Indianapolis: Indiana University Press.

164

PEIRCE, CHARLES SANDERS (1998) *The Essential Peirce, Volume 2: Selected Philosophical Writings (1893-1913)*, The Peirce Edition Project (ed.), Bloomington and Indianapolis: Indiana University Press.

PENG, F.C.C. (1985) "What is neurolinguistics?", in: *Journal of Neurolinguistics* 1 (1), pp. 7–30.

PERCHONOCK, NORMA AND OSWALD WERNER (1969) "Navaho systems of classification and some implications for ethnoscience", in: *Ethnology*, vol. 8, pp. 229–242.

PESSI, ANNE BIRGITTA (2008) "What Constitutes Experiences of Happiness and the Good Life? – Building a Novel Model on the Everyday Experiences", in: Heli Tissari, Anne Birgitta Pessi and Mikko Salmela (eds.), *Happiness: Cognition, Experience, Language. Collegium Studies across Disciplines in the Humanities and Social Sciences* 3, pp. 59–78, Helsinki: Helsinki Collegium for Advanced Studies.

PETERSON, CLIFFORD (ed.) (1977) *Saint Erkenwald*, Philadelphia: University of Pennsylvania Press.

PHILLIPS, COLIN, KUNIYOSHI L. SAKAI (2005) "Language and the brain", in: *Yearbook of Science and Technology*, Novi Eboraci: McGraw-Hill Publishers. pp. 166–169.

PLUMMER, C. AND J. EARLE (eds.) (1892; reprint 1952) *Two of the Saxon Chronicles*, vol. 1, pp. 29–234, Oxford: Oxford University Press.

PORZIG, WALTER (1928) "Sprachform und Bedeutung. Eine Auseinandersetzung mit A. Martys Sprachphilosophie", in: *Indogermanisches Jahrbuch, xii*, pp. 1–20.

PORZIG, WALTER (1934) "Wesenhafte Bedeutungsbeziehungen", in: *Beiträge zur Geschichte der deutsehen Sprache und Literatur* 58, pp. 70–79.

PORZIG, WALTER (2008) "Intrinsic Meaning Relations", in: Patrick Hanks (ed.), *Lexicology: Critical Concepts in Linguistics*, vol. 2, pp. 3–21, London, New York: Routledge (originally published as "Wesenhafte Bedeutungsbeziehungen", in: *Beiträge zur Geschichte der deutsehen Sprache und Literatur* 58 (1934): 70–97; trans. Elke Gehweiler).

POWELL, MARGARET JOYCE (ed.) (1916; reprint 1973) *The Pauline Epistles*, Kegan Paul, Trench, Trübner and Co.

QUINE, WILLARD VAN ORMAN (1987) *Quiddities: An Intermittently Philosophical Dictionary*, Cambridge, Mass.: Harvard University Press.

RADDEN, GÜNTER, KLAUS-MICHAEL KÖPCKE, THOMAS BERG AND PETER SIEMUND (2007) "The construction of meaning in language", in: Radden, Günter, Klaus-Michael Köpcke, Thomas Berg and Peter Siemund (eds.) *Aspects of Meaning Construction*, pp. 1–15, Amsterdam/Philadelphia: John Benjamins.

RAYEVSKA, N.M. (1979) *English Lexicology*, Kiev: 'Vyšča Škola' Publishers Head Publishing House.

RITCHIE, JOHN (1817) *The Scotsman, or Edinburgh political and literary journal*, Edinburgh.

ROSCH, ELEANOR (1975) "Cognitive representations of semantic categories", in: *Journal of Experimental Psychology, General* 104, pp. 193–233.

ROSSEAU, GEORGE. S. (1972) *Organic Form: The life of an idea*, London: Routledge & Kegan Paul.

RUSINEK, ANGELINA (2008a) "Clothes in the Network of CDs: The Case of Sweater", in: Robert Kiełtyka, Dorota Osuchowska, and Elżbieta Rokosz-Piejko (eds.), *Language, Literature, Culture and Beyond. Festschrift for Grzegorz A. Kleparski on his 50th Birthday*, pp. 138–145, Rzeszów: Wydawnictwo Uniwersytetu Rzeszowskiego.

RUSINEK, ANGELINA (2008b) "Clothes and People Go Together: A Historical Inquiry Into Crossing the Boundaries Between Conceptual Categories", *Studia Anglica Resoviensia* 5, pp. 125–138.

RUSINEK, ANGELINA (2009) "On the Non-Exclusiveness of Semantic Changes in the Category CLOTHES", in: Grzegorz A. Kleparski, Elżbieta Rokosz-Piejko, and Agnieszka Uberman (eds.), *Galicia English Teachings: Old Pitfalls, Changing Attitudes and New Vistas*, pp. 90–97, Rzeszów: Wydawnictwo Uniwersytetu Rzeszowskiego.

SAEED, JOHN J. (1997) *Semantics*, Oxford: Blackwell Publishers.

SALMELA, MIKKO (2008) "The Logical Structure of Joy (and Many Other Emotions)", in: Heli Tissari, Anne Birgitta Pessi and Mikko Salmela (eds.), *Happiness: Cognition, Experience, Language. Collegium Studies across Disciplines in the Humanities and Social Sciences* 3, pp. 23–40, Helsinki: Helsinki Collegium for Advanced Studies.

SAPIR, EDWARD (1921) *Language. An introduction to the study of speech*, New York: Harcourt, Brace and Company.

SAUSSURE DE, FERDINAND (1916) *Cours de linguistique générale*, Charles Bally and Albert Sechehaye (eds.), Lausanne and Paris: Payot (trans. W. Baskin, *Course in General Linguistics*, Glasgow: Fontana/Collins, 1977).

SAUSSURE DE, FERDINAND (1983) *Course in general linguistics*, translated and annotated by Roy Harris, London and New York: Bloomsbury.

SAWYER, PETER HAYES (1979) *Charters of Burton Abbey*, Oxford: Oxford University Press.

SCHREUDER, HINDRIK (1929) *Pejorative Sense Development in English*. College Park, Maryland: McGrath Publishing Company (reprint 1970).

Schuchardt, Hugo (1928) *Hugo Schuchardt-Brevier: Ein Vademecum der allgemeinen Sprachwissenschaft*, Leo Spitzer (ed.) 2nd ed. (1st ed., 1922), Halle/Saale: Niemeyer.

Schwarz, Hans (1959) "Leitmerkmale sprachliche Felder", in: *Sprache Schlüssel zur Welt*, Düsserdorf: Schwann, pp. 245–255.

Seymour, Michael C. and Gabriel M. Liegey, and others (eds.) (1975) *John Trevisa's Translation of Bartholomaeus Anglicus De Proprietatibus Rerum, a Critical Text*, vols. 1 and 2., Oxford: Clarendon.

Shakespeare, William (1600) *A midsommer nights dreame*, 1st Quarto, London: Thomas Fisher.

Sharma, Vinay Mohan (2005) *Body Language: The Art of Reading Gestures and Postures*, New Dehli: Pustak Mahal.

Shipley, Joseph T. (1955) *Dictionary of Early English*, New York: Philosophical Library.

Sihvola, Juha (2008) "Happiness in Ancient Philosophy", in: Heli Tissari, Anne Birgitta Pessi and Mikko Salmela (eds.), *Happiness: Cognition, Experience, Language. Collegium Studies across Disciplines in the Humanities and Social Sciences* 3, pp. 12–22, Helsinki: Helsinki Collegium for Advanced Studies.

Sisam, Kenneth (ed.) (1921; reprint 1933) *Fourteenth Century Verse and Prose*, pp. 169–70, London: Oxford University Press.

Skeat, Walter William (ed.) (1886; reprint 1973) *The Wars of Alexander, an Alliterative Romance*, pp. 23–25, 33–205, Dublin, Trinity College.

Smetana, Cyril Lawrence (ed.) (1977) *The Life of St. Norbert by John Capgrave*, pp. 21–155, Toronto: Pontifical Institute of Mediaeval Studies.

Smith, Lucy T. (ed.) (1885) *York Plays: The Plays Performed by the Crafts or Mysteries of York*, Oxford: Clarendon Press.

Spears, Richard A. (2000) *NTC's Dictionary of American Slang and Colloquial Expressions*, 3rd edition, NTC Publishing Group.

Spence, Nicol C. W. (1961) "Linguistic Fields, Conceptual Systems and the Weltbild", *Transactions of the Philological Society* 1961, pp. 87–106.

Sperber, Hans (1922) "Ein Gesetz der Bedeutungsentwicklung", in: *Zeitschrift fur deutsches Altertum*, 59, pp. 49–82.

spurgeongems = http://www.spurgeongems.org/vols25–27/chs1582.pdf

Stefanowitsch, Anatol (2006) "Words and their metaphors: A corpus-based approach", in: Anatol Stefanowitsch and Stefan Th. Gries (eds.), *Corpus-Based Approaches to Metaphor and Metonymy*, pp. 63–105, Berlin and New York: Mouton de Gruyter.

STERN, GUSTAF (1931) *Meaning and Change of Meaning, with Special Reference to the English Language,* Bloomington-London: Indiana University Press (reprint 1964).

STRAUSS, JÜRGEN (1986) "Concepts, fields, and 'non-basic' lexical items", in: Dieter Kastovsky and Aleksander Szwedek (eds.), *Linguistics across Historical and Geographical Boundaries: In Honour of Jacek Fisiak on the Occasion of His Fiftieth Birthday* Vol. 1, pp. 135–144, Berlin: Mouton de Gruyter.

SUMNER, LAURA (ed.) (1924) *The Weddynge of Sir Gawen and Dame Ragnell,* pp. 1–24, Northhampton, Massachusetts: Smith College Departments of Modern Languages.

SWEETSER, EVE (1990) *From Etymology to Pragmatics: Metaphorical and cultural aspects of semantic structure,* Cambridge: Cambridge University Press.

TAYLOR, JOHN R. (1989) *Linguistic Categorization: prototypes in Linguistic Theory.* 2nd edition, Oxford: Oxford University Press.

TAYLOR, JOHN R. (2002) *Cognitive Grammar,* New York: Oxford University Press.

Tee emm (Air Ministry training magazine, 1941–46 (2015) London: King's College.

TEGNÉR, ESAIAS (1874) *Spràk och nationalitet,* Stockholm: A. Bonnier.

TENNYSON, ALFRED (1842) *Poems,* London: Edward Moxon, 2 vols.

tfd = *the Free Dictionary,* http://www.thefreedictionary.com/

The Holy Bible: 1611 Edition, King James Version (1982) London: Thomas Nelson.

THORNE, TONY (2007) *Dictionary of Contemporary Slang,* 3rd edition, London: A&C Black.

THOMPSON, BARD (1996) *Humanists and Reformers: A History of the Renaissance and Reformation,* Cambridge: Wm. B. Eerdmans Publishing Co.

THORPE, BENJAMIN (1832) *Cædmon's Metrical Paraphrase Of Parts Of The Holy Scripture,* London: Society of Antiquaries of London.

THORPE, BENJAMIN (1842) *Codex Exoniensis,* London: Society of Antiquaries of London.

TISSARI, HELI (2008) "Happiness and Joy in Corpus Contexts: A Cognitive Semantic Analysis", in: Heli Tissari, Anne Birgitta Pessi and Mikko Salmela (eds.), *Happiness: Cognition, Experience, Language. Collegium Studies across Disciplines in the Humanities and Social Sciences* 3, pp. 144–174, Helsinki: Helsinki Collegium for Advanced Studies.

TOKARSKI, RYSZARD (1993) "Słownictwo jako interpretacja świata", in: J. Bartmiński (ed.), *Encyklopedia Kultury Polskiej XX Wieku,* Vol. 2, *Współczesny język polski,* Wrocław.

TOLKIEN, JOHN RONALD REUEL (ed.) (1962), *The English Text of the Ancrene Riwle: Ancrene Wisse: Edited from MS. Corpus Christi College, Cambridge 402, Early English Text Society 249*, Introduction by Neil Ripley Ker, London: Oxford University Press.

TRAUGOTT, ELIZABETH CLOSS AND RICHARD B. DASHER (2004) *Regularity in Semantic Change*, Cambridge: Cambridge University Press.

TRENCH, REV., RICHARD (1892) *The Study of Words*, Ann Arbor: Gryphon Books.

TRIER, JOST (1931) *Der deutsche Wortschatz im Sinnbezirk des Verstandes*, Heidelberg: Winter.

TRIER, JOST (1934) "Das sprachliche Feld: Eine Auseinandersetzung", in: *Neue Jahrbücher für Wissenschaft und Jegendbildung* 10, pp. 428–449.

TRIER, JOST (2008) "The Linguistic Field: An investigation", in: Patrick Hanks (ed.), *Lexicology: Critical Concepts in Linguistics*, vol. 2, pp. 22–44, London and New York: Routledge (originally published as "Das sprachliche Feld: Eine Auseinandersetzung", in: *Neue Jahrbücher für Wissenschaft und Jegendbildung* 10, pp. 428–449; trans. Elke Gehweiler and Patrick Hanks).

ULLMANN, STEPHEN (1957) *The Principles of Semantics*, Glasgow: Jackson, Son & Co.; Oxford: Basil Blackwell (2nd edition).

ULLMANN, STEPHEN (1972) "Semantics", in: Thomas A. Sebok (ed.), *Current Trends in Linguistics*, Hague: Mouton & Co. N.V.

UNGERER, FRIEDRICH AND HANS-JÖRG SCHMID (1996) *An Introduction to Cognitive Linguistics*, Harlow: Longman.

VASSILYEV, L.M. (1974) "The Theory of Semantic Fields: A survey", in: *Linguistics* 137, pp. 79–93.

WALDRON, RONALD A. (1967) *Sense and Sense Development*, London: Andre Deutsch (2nd edition).

WALDRON, TERENCE P. (1986) "Principles of language and mind", in: *Journal of Applied Psycholinguistics* 5, pp. 76–80.

WALLNER BJÖRN (1969, 1976, 1982, 1988) "The Middle English Translation of Guy de Chauliac's Grande Chirurgie, Lunds Universitets Arsskrift" in: *Acta Universitatis Lundensis*, Sectio I, Lund: Lund UP.

WARNER, R. D-N. (ed.) (1917; reprint 1971) *Early English Homilies from the Twelfth Century MS Vesp. D. xiv*, London: Oxford University Press, pp. 11–19.

WEISGERBER, LEO (1927) "Die Bedeutungslehre – ein Irrweg der Sprachwissenschaft?", in: *Germanisch-Romanische Monatsschrift* 15, pp. 161–183.

WEISGERBER, LEO (1962) *Sprachliche Gestaltung der Welt*, Düsseldorf: Schwann.

WHEATLEY, HENRY B. (ed.) (1865, 1866, 1869, 1899; reprint as two vols. 1987) *Merlin*, 4 vols., London: Early English Text Society/Oxford University Press.

Wierzbicka, Anna (1992) "Defining Emotion Concepts", in: *Cognitive Science* 16, pp. 539–581.

Wildgen, Wolfgang (2000) "The history and future of field semantics. From Giordano Bruno to dynamic semantics", in: Liliana Albertazzi, (ed.), *Meaning and Cognition*, pp. 203–226, Amsterdam and Philadelphia: John Benjamins.

Wittgenstein, Ludwig (1958) *Philosophical investigations*, (trans. Gertrude Elizabeth Margaret Anscombe), 2nd edition, Oxford: Blackwell.

Wright, William Aldis (ed.) (1873, 1878; reprint as one vol. 1987) *Generydes*, London: Early English Text Society/Oxford University Press.

Wright, William Aldis (ed.) (1887) *The Metrical Chronicle of Robert of Gloucester*, 2 vols., Rolls Series 86, London: Spottiswoode.

Zettersten, Arne (ed.) (1976) *The English Text of the Ancrene Riwle: Magdalene College Cambridge MS Pepys 2498*, pp. 1–201, London: Oxford University Press.

Żyśko, Konrad and Angelina Żyśko (in preparation) "What's in the Name?: A Cognitive Contrastive Analysis of Compounded English, Spanish and Polish Animal Names"

Index

Sounds – Meaning – Communication

Landmarks in Phonetics, Phonology and Cognitive Linguistics

Edited by Jolanta Szpyra-Kozłowska

Vol.   1   Hubert Kowalewski: Motivating the Symbolic. Towards a Cognitive Theory of the Linguistic Sign. 2016.

Vol.   2   Jolanta Szpyra-Kozłowska / Eugeniusz Cyran (eds.): Phonology, its Faces and Interfaces. 2016.

Vol.   3   Angelina Żyśko: English 'Joyful' Vocabulary – Semantic Developments. 2016.

www.peterlang.com